"For generations God's inerrant Word has brought light and life into the hearts of men and women worldwide. In this timely seventy-fifth anniversary devotional by Wycliffe, you will be privileged to be the beneficiary of that same life-giving experience."

— **Dr. Tony Evans**, senior pastor of Oak Cliff Bible Fellowship and president of The Urban Alternative

———————

"This devotional book is beautiful and makes the Word of God come alive! The stories will take you to places all over the globe and reaffirm the transcendence of the Scriptures to all peoples and all cultures. The visuals are stunning and a perfect reflection of God's creation! Sink deeply into this book. It will lift your spirits and give you strength for the journey."

— **Rev. Dr. Brenda Salter McNeil**, author of *Roadmap to Reconciliation*

———————

"It's amazing when a devotional so perfectly can remind us of both the personal and global aspects of the transforming power of the TRUTH found in God's Word. This one does that! My husband and I love it!"

— **Becky Hunter**, former president of the Global Pastors Wives Network, author of *Being Good to Your Husband on Purpose* and *Why Her? You, Your Daughter-in-Law and the Big Picture*, and wife to Dr. Joel Hunter, senior pastor of Northland, A Church Distributed

WHEN GOD'S WORD SPEAKS

© 2016 by Wycliffe Bible Translators, Inc.

Cover design by Ben Rupp. Cover photo by Rodney Ballard.

ISBN: 978-0-938978-51-0

Printed in the United States of America.

First printing 2016 by Wycliffe Bible Translators, Inc.

INTRODUCTION BY BOB CRESON

WHEN
God's Word
SPEAKS

**STORIES OF THE POWER OF SCRIPTURE
IN THE LIVES OF GOD'S PEOPLE TODAY**

Wycliffe®
BibleTranslators

CONTENTS

INTRODUCTION

There is great power in God's Word. We can easily point to the historical significance of the Bible, but often we need to be reminded of the power it can have in our lives today.

William Cameron Townsend (Cam), the founder of Wycliffe Bible Translators, had a profound understanding of that power. The Bible had transformed his life, and he believed it would do the same for others both in the United States and around the world.

"I've built my whole life around that book, God's Word to us," he said.

This wasn't a new concept, but God planned Cam's vision to be the jet fuel for global Bible translation. Thousands of language groups all over the world were waiting to understand God's message for them. Cam dedicated many years of his life to helping bring it to them, and he had countless stories about how God shaped and refined his faith during that time. (You'll find one of those stories at the end of this book!)

From the largest to the smallest people groups on earth, every man, woman, and child has a right to the Word of God. No one should have to learn another language to understand it.

Cam stood on the shoulders of John Wycliffe, William Tyndale, Martin Luther, and others who believed that Scripture—God's Word in people's hands, written clearly, accurately, and naturally in a language they can clearly understand—can transform lives.

It's hard to believe it's been seventy-five years since God entrusted Cam with the task to mobilize people to translate his Word all over the world, and Wycliffe Bible Translators was born. Fast-forward to today, and we remain in awe of the power of God's Word in the lives of his people.

This collection of stories includes accounts from people all over the world—missionaries, successful executives, seasoned pastors, Bible translators, and communities encountering Scripture for the very first time. It highlights moments when God used his Word to speak into someone's heart and bring transformation, and it celebrates the incredible importance of the Bible in growing and shaping God's kingdom today.

May you be refreshed by the verses and passages, inspired by each story, and comforted and encouraged by reminders of God's power to move in us and through us for his glory. Discover how the Word of God is alive and active today.

Bob Creson

For you have been born again, but not to a life that will quickly end. Your new life will last forever because it comes from the eternal, living word of God. As the Scriptures say, "People are like grass; their beauty is like a flower in the field. The grass withers and the flower fades. But the word of the Lord remains forever." And that word is the Good News that was preached to you.

— 1 PETER 1:23-25

In the beginning the Word already existed

THE WORD WAS WITH GOD
AND THE WORD
WAS GOD

— JOHN 1:1

*pre shiin pre we pe
wejikaara numu.*
[17]La, ŋmba na o Tafun pie
mbra kre, wre na wre we pe
nunu ŋumu nu.
[18]E tiɛrɛɛ ti, sisaa ŋga
lewo pini kpan kra u wejinge
kla, la, ŋmba u tirri kre, u
sisaa pini na u wejinge klai,
[19]E chin na e wejinge pe
kpra Ɗumu wre nyimgɛs, a
Nyiɛkpɔɔ wre wre s use a
wi. a ʼsʼ svn se ... Nyiɛkpɔɔ
mu ʼbus se ʼ sn we lenge,

...sto Leele Yɛtaara
Kaari Sisaa Pee
ʼre yo mbo, "Koloo
i jaa kee ŋga ni
e." Pan ki nyi ya.
ma ki nyu mu mu
aa yo na nii kole
e ŋga ni chaa
ba ti mbe kee ka
lejuŋo we yo

Quest for Solid Ground

In the beginning the Word already existed. The Word was with God, and the Word was God. He existed in the beginning with God. God created everything through him, and nothing was created except through him. The Word gave life to everything that was created, and his life brought light to everyone. The light shines in the darkness, and the darkness can never extinguish it.

— John 1:1–5

I love that old hymn, "My Hope Is Built on Nothing Less." The first verse is by far my favorite:

> *My hope is built on nothing less*
> *Than Jesus' blood and righteousness;*
> *I dare not trust the sweetest frame,*
> *But wholly lean on Jesus' name.*
> *On Christ, the solid Rock, I stand;*
> *All other ground is sinking sand.*

Solid ground. That's what the Word of God provides for us. All Scripture points to Christ. Are you like me in wanting a deep understanding of your identity in Jesus? He is our grace-filled and normative guidance.

The last verse of that great hymn says:

> *When he shall come with trumpet sound,*
> *Oh, may I then in him be found,*
> *Clothed in his righteousness alone,*
> *Faultless to stand before the throne!*
> *On Christ, the solid Rock, I stand;*
> *All other ground is sinking sand.*

The solid Rock is Christ Jesus. He is both God and the very Word of God who, for a time, entered into our human experience.

I hope you value this Word. Scripture tells us, "In the beginning the Word already existed. The Word was with God, and the Word was God. He existed in the beginning with God. God created everything through him, and nothing was created except through him. The Word gave life to everything that was created, and his life brought light to everyone. The light shines in the darkness, and the darkness can never extinguish it. . . . So the Word became human and made his home among us. He was full of unfailing love and faithfulness. And we have seen his glory, the glory of the Father's one and only Son" (John 1:1-5, 14).

I love Eugene Peterson's interpretation of this last verse: "The Word became flesh and blood, and moved into the neighborhood" (John 1:14a, The Message). God entered our world through Jesus, and he revealed himself compassionately in the midst of outcasts.

For the peoples of the earth, and, yes, for you and me, this is good news—the Good News about Jesus Christ.

— Bob Creson

YOUR VERY LIVES ARE A *LETTER* THAT ANYONE CAN READ BY JUST LOOKING AT YOU CHRIST HIMSELF WROTE IT — NOT WITH INK BUT WITH *GOD'S* LIVING SPIRIT NOT CHISELED INTO STONE BUT CARVED INTO HUMAN LIVES — AND WE PUBLISH *it*

— 2 CORINTHIANS 3:2-3 (THE MESSAGE)

This Book Is Alive

Your very lives are a letter that anyone can read by just looking at you. Christ himself wrote it—not with ink, but with God's living Spirit, not chiseled into stone, but carved into human lives—and we publish it.

— 2 Corinthians 3:2–3 (The Message)

This Book is alive. The Word of God changes lives. It changed mine!

In 1998, I attended a ceremony celebrating the completion of the Eastern Jacaltec New Testament translation in Guatemala. I was privileged to help fund the printing of the New Testament, which is why I was invited to the celebration. On the way to the celebration I learned that the translation was begun in 1958. I was born in 1961, so I couldn't fathom waiting that long for anything.

The ceremony made a deep impression on me, especially when I saw Gaspar, one of the Eastern Jacaltec translators, weep uncontrollably as he received his copy of the New Testament. I was stunned!

That night, in a cold hotel room, I found myself unable to sleep. I began to read Kay Arthur's book *As Silver Refined* and came upon these words: "Being in God's Word and knowing it for yourself is the key."

My mind flashed back to the celebration and the image of Gaspar, the primary translator for the New Testament, weeping as for the first time he clutched the Word of God in a language he could clearly understand. "Here I am," I said to myself, "a

third-generation Christian on one side and a fifth-generation Christian on the other. I sell Bibles as my business. I've sold thousands of Bibles, but I've never before seen anyone weep when I sold them a Bible!"

And then I thought about my own life. "I have forty or fifty Bibles in my home, but I don't read the Bible regularly," I thought.

It was a turning point for me. God brought conviction to my heart, and during the wee hours of February 8, 1998, I promised God that every morning thereafter I would rise and begin my day by reading his Word. I haven't missed a day since, and the Word has spoken to my heart many, many times. Now my passion is to instill that same love of the Word in others.

— Mart Green

"Being in God's Word and knowing it for yourself is the key."

JESUS TOLD HIM

I

AM

THE

WAY

— JOHN 14:6

Straw Hats

Jesus told him, "I am the way, the truth, and the life. No one can come to the Father except through me."

— John 14:6

I arrived at the Tlapa market in Mexico looking for a guide and hired a man wearing three colorful hats. He had bought the hats with money earned from selling goods. Wanting to keep them clean and undamaged, he'd placed them, one on top of the other, over the old dingy hat he was already wearing.

Those colored straw hats would save my life.

I made it clear to the guide that I was in a hurry, eager to make it to my destination in one long day rather than the usual two. By two o'clock in the morning we were up and on our way. Without a word, my guide slung our bedrolls on top of his pack, jammed all three hats onto his head, and disappeared into the darkness. Perfect! No dillydallying with this man!

I finally caught up and fell in line behind him. I could see absolutely nothing in the pitch-blackness of a moonless night. Nothing, that is, except the outline of those new straw hats.

Soon we were climbing. The trail quickly narrowed until we were on a ledge high on the sheer mountainside. I was puffing and straining to keep up. I heard a noise behind me and turned my head to see what it was. At that instant I stepped off into space and felt myself falling.

Instinctively I threw my hands out ahead of me into the darkness. Somehow my elbows caught on a ledge, and my body swung in tight against the rock wall beneath. I hung there until the guide grabbed my arms and hauled me to safety.

The trail had taken a sharp v-shaped jog. In turning my head, I had taken my eyes off the straw hats and, instead of stepping left as the guide had done, I stepped straight into the void! Believe me, after that I did not take my eyes off those straw hats again until daybreak—some four hours later.

My guide had been over this trail hundreds of times, so he knew every step, every turn, and every rock; it seemed like he could see in the dark. I, on the other hand, did not know the way. It was far smarter to trust him. So I kept my eyes on those straw hats and waited for the dawn.

Later that day a Bible verse that I'd memorized years before came to mind. This experience gave it new meaning. Jesus said, "I am the way. . . . No one can come to the Father except through me" (John 14:6). Jesus has the road map. He does not tell us about the way, and then leave us to find it. He's our guide in the dark on a treacherous trail, and we have his Word, which we're told is a lamp to guide our feet and a light for our path (Ps. 119:105).

Our life going forward is an unknown path. We've never been this direction before, so how can we know the way? God knows, and he sent Jesus Christ not only to show the way but also to become the Way. Put yourself in the hands of the only available and trustworthy guide, Jesus Christ. You'll find him completely dependable.

— George Cowan

spiritual
wisdom
&
understanding

Seeing from God's Point of View

*We ask God to give you complete knowledge of his will and to give
you spiritual wisdom and understanding.*

— Colossians 1:9b

My wife, Linda, and I used to work as linguists and Bible translators in Brazil. Sometimes the men in the village where we lived would take me hunting with them. While out on an expedition, I asked one of the hunters how they could see so many things in the forest. Typically I never saw what they were hunting until after they'd killed it.

The hunter replied, "Steve, your problem is that the things you see are very small [that is, you see only a few things]. Even with an extra set of eyes [your glasses], you don't see what's important. You don't see well because you only try to see with your eyes. We, on the other hand, have very large vision [we see many things]. We see things you don't. For example, we see the colorful macaw parrot with our eyes. Wild pigs and monkeys, we see with our ears [we hear their noise]. We see the anteater with our noses [we smell their odor]. We see snakes with our skin, because they make us tingle when we sense they're near. And the sky, stars, sun, and moon, which reflect the passage of time, we see from the inside out, and all over."

Growing up in their magnificent rainforest, these hunters learned to sense the invisible things around them and find meaning in what their senses told them. They recognized the sound of a wild pig, for instance, and the odor of an anteater.

As Linda and I thought about how the people described seeing the world around them, we prayed that they—and we—would see God in his creation. As Romans 1:20a says, "Ever since the world was created, people have seen the earth and sky. Through everything God made, they can clearly see his invisible qualities—his eternal power and divine nature."

At the same time, we found ourselves challenged in another way. How well did we "see" spiritually? J. B. Phillips translates Colossians 1:9b this way, "We are asking God that you may see things, as it were, from his point of view by being given spiritual insight and understanding" (Phillips).

I am grateful that God lets us see his eternal power and divine nature through all he has created. I am also challenged to ask God daily to help me learn his ways through his Word, so that I will consistently see people and events from his point of view and understand them with clear spiritual vision.

— Steve Sheldon

All Scripture

— *is* —

[inspired]

BY GOD

— 2 TIMOTHY 3:16

Inspired by God

All Scripture is inspired by God and is useful to teach us what is true and to make us realize what is wrong in our lives.

— 2 Timothy 3:16a

No word in Scripture is unimportant. There isn't anything God wants to say that he cannot say in a clear and natural way in any language he wants to. And no one is too unimportant to merit the Scriptures in the language they understand best.

Bible translation respects the people receiving the Scriptures, and through the process, it frees them to have a relationship with God in their own words.

In Nigeria, the Mbe translation team was translating the Gospel of Luke. They came to chapter 2, verse 7, which says, "She [Mary] gave birth to her firstborn son. She wrapped him snugly in strips of cloth and laid him in a manger, because there was no lodging available for them."

The translators took the time to ponder how to translate some of the words, but not "manger." They immediately used the word *ókpáng*.

As their translation consultant, I asked them, "What's an *ókpáng*? Tell me what it looks like." One of the translators drew a picture on the whiteboard. It was essentially a cradle hung by ropes so that the newborn could be laid in it and swung.

I suggested they check the collection of notes and commentaries we were using to help the translators whose first language isn't English. The Mbe translators saw that "manger" referred to an animal-feeding trough.

Even as the Mbe team read the notes, they objected. "We have always used the word *ókpáng*. We have used it for years, and that's what we should use." I pointed out to them that it wasn't just a matter of tradition. God expects us to find the words that express the original meaning as accurately as possible. Furthermore, this word tells us something profound about God.

"When he came to live among us and bring salvation to us, he came in the lowliest way possible. He did not come and sleep in a nice *ókpáng* like every Mbe mother wants for her newborn. Instead, he showed us his unbelievable humility," I told them. "So we need to find your best word for an animal-feeding trough."

Suddenly the person who had argued most loudly for the traditional term offered, "We feed our animals out of an old worn-out basket that isn't usable anymore, except to feed the animals. We call it *édzábrí*.'"

"Then try that term," I said.

As the Mbe people listened, they were visibly moved. Picturing the newborn baby lying in the animals' feeding basket, they recognized in a new way that Jesus was willing to do whatever it took to reach them. As an adult, he would humble himself by washing the disciples' feet and then by dying on the cross. And this humility started right from birth, when he was born to a young peasant woman under questionable social conditions and laid in an animal-feeding trough.

God in Jesus entered our world. The Word became human and made his home with us (John 1:14). He entered our space, identifying with our weakness, sorrow, grief, and our sin even though he himself did not sin.

— John Watters

IF WE DON'T LOVE PEOPLE WE CAN SEE, HOW CAN WE LOVE GOD, WHOM WE CANNOT SEE?

— 1 JOHN 4:20

I Am a Liar

If someone says, "I love God," but hates a fellow believer, that person is a liar; for if we don't love people we can see, how can we love God, whom we cannot see?

— 1 John 4:20

Isn't it easy to sing praises to God on Sunday morning in church? But what about in daily life when we get hurt, criticized, or rejected by a brother or sister? Can we still keep Jesus's command in John 13:34b, "Just as I have loved you, you should love each other"? Or are we in danger of even hating such a brother or sister?

When my husband and I worked on translation with the Inupiaq people in Alaska, we put into use New Testament Scriptures that a consultant had already checked. We copied passages from those books for Sunday evening services. I asked different people each time if they would like to read a passage, but I didn't know who would be available because the Inupiaq people travel often. I prayed that I would give each text to the right person.

On one occasion I asked an Inupiaq woman named Daphne to read. She agreed and went up to the pulpit that next Sunday. Before she started to read the text she said, "I practiced all week so I would read well tonight, but this text really bothered me: 'If we say we love God and hate our brother, we are liars'. So I am a liar," she continued. "I don't love everyone here. Please forgive me. I want to love everybody. I don't want to be a liar. I love God, and I want to love you all."

What a tremendous testimony! Daphne had probably been a Christian for more than thirty years, but she had never fully understood the Bible in English. It spoke to her heart in her Inupiaq language. Another friend who had not been at this service said later on, "Daphne is different now."

So whenever we are hurt or criticized by someone, let's pray right away, "Lord, give me love and the ability to forgive." It's amazing how the Lord answers so that no bitterness is left, and we can be his true disciples.

— Hildegard Seiler

> *"I don't love everyone here. Please forgive me. I want to love everybody. I don't want to be a liar."*

YOU TURNED AWAY FROM

IDOLS

The Day the Teacher Learned a Lesson

For they keep talking about the wonderful welcome you gave us and how you turned away from idols to serve the living and true God.

— 1 Thessalonians 1:9

"What is God saying to you in this chapter?" I asked Jaco, my Canela-speaking friend and best translation helper. His answer astounded me.

He'd told me a few days before that he had recently started following Jesus. Wow! The first believer! Now I was having the first lesson with this young brother in Christ about how to have morning devotions. In case he needed some help, I had picked out a couple of meaningful statements from the passage and jotted them down to "prime the pump."

I asked Jaco to read aloud the first chapter of the recently printed letter of 1 Thessalonians. He did, and that's when I asked my question, "What is God saying to you in this chapter?"

"Oh, the idea in verse 9, of course!" Jaco replied. "That's the best verse in the whole chapter!"

What? I hadn't even noticed anything in verse 9; it sure wasn't on my "prime the pump" list of ideas! Jaco explained, "Paul is happy with those Jesus followers in Thessalonica because they turned away from the dead, fake gods to serve our living Father!"

"Yes, that's nice," I said. "But what about it?" I still hadn't caught on.

"Look, they are just like me!" Jaco said. "I turned away from the ghosts of the dead ancestors, away from the spirits of dead beings, and turned toward our Father, who is alive. I don't need to concern myself with dead things anymore, but with a living Father!"

Of course! How could I have been so dumb? I knew that the Canelas, in accordance with their community's traditional religion, lived in fear of the ghosts of the dead, constantly seeking to placate them by practicing age-old ceremonies and rituals.

It was a lesson to me from God himself. "My Holy Spirit is well able to teach young Canela believers directly from my Word," I heard him telling me. "Keep on translating my Word into their language so I can speak personally to them."

I did. Ten years later the Scriptures were dedicated, and the Canela church was established.

Are there "dead, fake gods" in your life that are keeping you from serving our living Father?

— Jack Popjes

THE LORD IS MY SHEPHERD; I HAVE ALL THAT I NEED. HE LETS ME REST IN GREEN MEADOWS; HE LEADS ME BESIDE PEACEFUL STREAMS. HE RENEWS MY STRENGTH. HE GUIDES ME ALONG RIGHT PATHS, BRINGING HONOR TO HIS NAME. EVEN WHEN I WALK THROUGH THE DARKEST VALLEY, I WILL NOT BE AFRAID, FOR YOU ARE CLOSE BESIDE ME. YOUR ROD AND YOUR STAFF PROTECT AND COMFORT **ME**

— PSALM 23:1-4

The Faith of a Goatherd

The LORD is my shepherd; I have all that I need. He lets me rest in green meadows; he leads me beside peaceful streams. He renews my strength. He guides me along right paths, bringing honor to his name. Even when I walk through the darkest valley, I will not be afraid, for you are close beside me. Your rod and your staff protect and comfort me.

— Psalm 23:1–4

While I was teaching at a Bible college in Mozambique, we were reading Psalm 23 for our devotional. I expected all the pastoral candidates to be as familiar with the verses as I am. The candidates read through the passage, and I realized it meant something different to them than it did to me.

I was touched by the comments of Ilidio, a young man from the Nyungwe people group. Ilidio grew up in the dry, rocky, hot part of Mozambique that his community calls home. With limited water, crops often fail, but Nyungwes are expert herdsmen. Most Nyungwe boys like Ilidio herd goats from about the age of ten.

We were about to close our study time when he spoke up. "When I walk through the darkest valley, I will not be afraid. . . . Your rod and your staff protect and comfort me," he read.

"When I was a boy herding goats, they followed me anywhere, even through rocky places where snakes or lions could be hiding. They knew that if I walked ahead with the stick, they were safe," he said. "I wouldn't lead them into danger. I would defend them with the stick if there was a problem. They trusted me completely. We need to be like that with God."

Well said. Now I read these verses with the deeper understanding given to me by a Nyungwe goatherd who has chosen to translate the Bible for his people.

— Jeni Bister

"They trusted me completely. We need to be like that with God."

THOUGH YOU DO NOT SEE HIM NOW

you trust him

— 1 PETER 1:8

A Voice in the Storm

You love him even though you have never seen him. Though you do not see him now, you trust him; and you rejoice with a glorious, inexpressible joy.

— 1 Peter 1:8

The controller's calm voice filled the cockpit of my small twin-engine Cessna airplane.

"One engine has failed," he confirmed from Houston Center. "We have you on radar. Montgomery County Airport is forty-five miles southeast of your position. Would you like vectors?"

For the last half hour I had been enjoying the bright Texas sky as we cruised high above the clouds. Below us, rain and fog blanketed the ground between Dallas and our destination, Houston. Then, BANG! One engine on the Cessna sputtered and stopped. The dead prop on my right looked strange and ominous. I could still fly—one of the joys of twin engines—but I was not overly ecstatic about making a single-engine approach into an unknown airport in weather that had the ducks walking.

I glanced over at my two passengers. They were staring, transfixed, at the motionless propeller.

"We'll soon be on the ground at another airport," I said, in a weak effort to allay their anxieties. But who was around to comfort me? I reached for the microphone, and soon the Houston controller made contact.

"Okay, Houston," I responded. "I'm with you. Requesting vectors to Montgomery Airport."

"Turn left," he said, "heading 110 degrees. Descend to 4,000 feet."

I followed his directions implicitly, trying to keep the airplane trim and level at the same time. At 4,000 feet we entered the clouds, flying blind through the mist and rain.

"Descend to 3,000 feet and turn left 5 degrees. Now turn right 30 degrees and descend to 1,500 feet."

As we dipped into the rain clouds, I could barely see the tip of my wing. But I knew that he knew where I was. That was enough. I didn't know his name. I had never seen his face. But I knew I could trust him. I had no other choice—unless I wanted to try and make it on my own.

Suddenly we broke out of the clouds and there it was, a mile of wet asphalt glistening in the rain. I'd never known asphalt to look so beautiful.

I'd been more than willing to entrust my life to a faceless voice speaking complex directions through the fog. Touching down, I thought of another voice. Calm, patient, ever present when over the years blinding mists have thrown carefully wrought plans into chaos. His voice.

Did I really trust that voice? Did I trust God as much as I trusted the stranger in Houston? Would I be willing to follow exacting instructions when I couldn't see any farther than the end of my nose?

Good questions—questions we have to answer daily.

— Bernie May

Oh THAT YOU WOULD CHOOSE *life*

— DEUTERONOMY 30:19

The Power of Blessing

*Oh, that you would choose life, so that you and your descendants might live! You can make this choice by loving the L*ORD *your God, obeying him, and committing yourself firmly to him. This is the key to your life.*

— Deuteronomy 30:19b–20a

"He's dying! My brother is dying," Konime, a pastor in Papua New Guinea, told my husband and me. He was convinced his brother, Mahki, would die because someone had put a curse on him.

Pastor Konime led us to a dark hut where we found Mahki lying on a mat, unable to walk and barely able to speak. "He won't eat the food I bring him," his wife tearfully confided.

It was true, we concluded. He would die unless God intervened.

We asked Mahki if we could pray for him. He lifted his head slightly and nodded.

We cried out to our heavenly Father, asking him to intervene for Mahki. We spoke the words of Deuteronomy 30:19–20. We chose life and blessing for Mahki, "Lord, cause him to also choose life over death, your blessing over the enemy's curse."

We spoke a blessing over Mahki, "Lord, we know you want to bless your child Mahki. And we bless him." Last, we rebuked the curse.

Exhausted but feeling the battle won, we sat quietly in expectation of what God would do. We watched with thanksgiving to our miracle-working God as Mahki slowly sat up. He looked up and gave us a weak smile. Before we left, his delighted wife brought him food, and he began to eat.

A literal hands-on experience that day taught us how exceedingly powerful a curse is. We also realized in contrast that if a curse is this powerful, how much more powerful is a blessing when given in the name of Jesus Christ!

Later we met Mahki's daughter who told us, "Shortly after you prayed for my father, he was open to receiving Jesus. My uncle, Pastor Konime, had the joy of leading his brother to the Lord and then baptizing him!"

— Aretta Loving

"Lord, cause him to also choose life over death, your blessing over the enemy's curse."

We destroy
every proud obstacle
that keeps people from

knowing

GOD

— 2 CORINTHIANS 10:5

I Am, the Hero

We destroy every proud obstacle that keeps people from knowing God. We capture their rebellious thoughts and teach them to obey Christ.

— 2 Corinthians 10:5

Maybe Paul's military imagery in this section of 2 Corinthians inspires the heart of every young man, but as I was a new recruit to Wycliffe Bible Translators, this verse became sort of my "war cry."

I had heard the stories of warrior missionaries who persisted through cultural stresses and hardship, devoting their entire lives to translating the Bible so others could understand it clearly. I had seen the videos of these godly legends celebrating the completion of a New Testament in a local language. The excitement was contagious. The war was on! I couldn't wait! I was ready to take on the enemy and demolish his strongholds.

However, after missionary training, language learning, and five years spent surveying the language group I would serve, when my team was finally ready to begin our actual translation work, we were told that it might be better to start training other coworkers instead.

"No way," I thought. "That wasn't the plan, God!" I resisted our leaders, who wanted us to move in this direction. I made excuses. I followed my own plans. I wanted the Bible translator to be me, not someone else. I didn't want to train others. I wanted to be the hero!

And there it was—my huge ego staring back at me, my desire to be the hero. I started seeing it all over the place. When I looked back at previous newsletters I'd sent home, references to me, myself, and I stood out like a white missionary in the village marketplace. "My work," "my language program," "my people." I gave, I preached, I witnessed. In the village, I was a star. "You're so tall," people often told me. "You speak our language." "You're so smart." Even when I returned home for a break on furlough, my ego had a feast. "Your commitment is astounding," friends and family gushed. "I admire your sacrifice." "You're an example to all of us."

I hadn't done a good job applying 2 Corinthians 10:5 to my own life. My ego was a proud obstacle—a high thing that rose up against God. I didn't capture those arrogant thoughts and lead them into captivity. I had my own plan, but God is the only one who orchestrates the salvation of others. Thankfully he continues to work on me and lets me be a part of his plan. I am not the hero; I Am is the hero.

— Jim Meyers

JESUS REPLIED

I AM THE BREAD OF LIFE

WHOEVER COMES TO ME

WILL NEVER BE HUNGRY AGAIN

WHOEVER BELIEVES IN ME

WILL NEVER BE THIRSTY

— JOHN 6:35

The Bread of Life

Jesus replied, "I am the bread of life. Whoever comes to me will never be hungry again. Whoever believes in me will never be thirsty."

— John 6:35

"How do you explain Jesus as the bread of life to someone with no concept of bread?"

That was the rhetorical question thrown my way by a Bible professor on my first trip to Africa. We were learning about Bible translation efforts in the Congo—a country that had been ravaged by decades of civil conflict, resulting in thousands of displaced refugees.

I knew what bread was. I understood it as a food staple. I could comprehend what Jesus meant when he said that he was the "bread of life," because it all made sense in my language and culture. But how does someone understand that when there is no bread?

The professor's question rang in my ears like a blast from a cannon. For more than two decades I had read the Bible, never appreciating the work that took place centuries ago to bring God's Word into the language of the common English speaker. Now I was halfway around the world meeting people who had never enjoyed the "bread" that I'd been given.

The words of Christ took on a whole new level of importance. "I am the bread of life. Whoever comes to me will never be hungry again" (John 6:35).

Suddenly the faces of those who were still hungry for this bread looked eerily familiar. It was the face of the man who had helped us get our bags off the airplane when we landed on the dusty airstrip to begin our time in Africa. It was the face of the woman at the hotel who checked us in to our rooms. It was the face of the student studying to be a Bible translator for his own language community at the university where we were working.

For them, maybe Jesus is the rice of life. Perhaps he is the tortilla. Or he might be the cassava of life. Whatever he is, they need him. They need him just as much as I need my own bread of life.

Today, several years removed from that encounter in the Congo, the verse hangs on the wall of my kitchen. It serves as a reminder of Jesus's provision in my life and the spiritual hunger that still exists for those who have never heard of him.

— Dustin Moody

> For them, maybe Jesus is the rice of life. Perhaps he is the tortilla. Or he might be the cassava of life. Whatever he is, they need him.

Those who have never been told
about him will

see

and those who have never heard
of him will

understand

— ROMANS 15:21

Those Who Have Never Been Told

I have been following the plan spoken of in the Scriptures, where it says,
"Those who have never been told about him will see, and those who have never
heard of him will understand."

— Romans 15:21

Faith comes from hearing the Good News about Christ. Paul said, "My ambition has always been to preach the Good News where the name of Christ has never been heard, rather than where a church has already been started by someone else. I have been following the plan spoken of in the Scriptures, where it says, 'Those who have never been told about him will see, and those who have never heard of him will understand'" (Rom. 15:20-21).

In another instance Paul reminds the Romans, "'Everyone who calls on the name of the Lord will be saved.' But how can they call on him to save them unless they believe in him? And how can they believe in him if they have never heard about him? And how can they hear about him unless someone tells them?" (Rom. 10:13-14).

Now, not everyone welcomes the message, but that isn't our work; that's the work of the Holy Spirit. We are salt and light, but it's not our choice when God uses us for that purpose. That's his choice alone. Our work is to stay focused on Christ—to know nothing but him. We don't need to use lofty words and impressive wisdom to tell about God's plan. The message can and should be very plain. We can rely on God's Spirit and power, not on our human wisdom.

And this is the Good News: Motivated by his love for the people of this world, God gave his one and only Son, so that everyone who calls on his name, everyone who believes in him, will not perish but have eternal life. God sent his Son into the world not to judge the world, but to save the world through him.

We are here for the sake of others! May God remind us always that, like Paul, we are to proclaim the Good News where the name of Christ has never been proclaimed.

God, your Word is more precious than all I possess. It gives light to my path and directs my steps. Because of your grace, and by the power of your Word, minds are transformed and lives renewed. I now pray for all people who don't yet know you. You've promised that every tribe, people, and nation will hear your voice, so equip me to do my part to help everyone who needs your eternal Word.

— Bob Creson

We can rely on God's Spirit and power, not on our human wisdom.

I have put my hope in *your* **WORD**

— PSALM 119:81

Delivering Hope

I am worn out waiting for your rescue, but I have put my hope in your word.

— Psalm 119:81

As we circled the grass airstrip, I was anxious that we were going to disappoint the people waiting to greet us. These dear people had been living in a war zone for many years. For the past eighteen months their town had been occupied by government troops while being simultaneously under siege by rebel forces.

They had lost three successive crops to the fighting forces, and hunger was their main diet. There had been no medical supplies in the town for several years. Even normal commerce had ceased, and peoples' clothing was literally wearing out. It would be very understandable for the welcoming party to expect us to be flying in food, medicines, or clothing.

Seven years earlier we had three translation teams and a group of literacy trainers and specialists living there. But with the escalation of the war, all our staff had left for other towns and countries. In the intervening seven years, the Bible translations had continued with displaced refugee communities from those three languages.

Portions of Scripture had been completed and published. Scripture songs were composed by the refugee communities and published in songbooks. There were alphabet books, primers, and storybooks in all three languages.

One of the translators and I had hatched a plan to make the first visit to the town in seven years. Since it was still technically a war zone, we would hire a single-engine charter plane, fly along the border to the closest point to the town, and then make a brief low-altitude flight across the border. There the pilot would land, drop us off, and then return for us three days later.

As the translator and I put together the load of goods we would take with us, we were limited to a total cargo weight of less than two hundred pounds. We wanted to take the Scripture portions, the songbooks, and the reading materials with us, but two small footlockers of those filled our entire cargo allowance. We knew people were hungry, sick, and naked. Did we dare to not take food, medicines, and clothing? Finally we decided that while others might bring in those goods, only we could bring in the newly published sections of God's Word.

So there we were, circling the airstrip, and I was worried about letting our friends down by not bringing things for their physical needs. As we disembarked from the plane, the welcoming party came forward, shook our hands, and greeted us effusively. Then they asked us, "Did you bring us Bibles?"

I have often reflected on that moment. If I were hungry and ill and naked, would I seek my physical needs more than my spiritual needs? The war had stripped our friends of all their worldly possessions, but somehow they managed to keep their priorities straight.

— Russ Hersman

He struck the water
with Elijah's cloak
and cried out

Where is the Lord
the God of Elijah?

Then the river divided
and Elisha went across

— 2 KINGS 2:14

Not *Why*, but *Where*?

He struck the water with Elijah's cloak and cried out, "Where is the LORD, the God of Elijah?" Then the river divided, and Elisha went across.

— 2 Kings 2:14

One of the hardest words to acquire during our early years of language learning among the Amanab people of Papua New Guinea was the word *why*. The Amanab people value community, working together, and things remaining the same. They use *why* only in a critical manner, like one would scold a child who broke a vase: "Why did you do that?"

One warm December morning we watched a close Amanab friend die before our eyes. Back in my house in anger and sorrow, I yelled at God, "Why, God? Why did you let her die?" Almost immediately I sensed God asking, "Andy, what did the Amanab teach you about *why*?" I was upset by the question, but as I thought about it, I responded, "I guess in Amanab, you only use *why* to be critical of someone."

In essence I was not asking to understand God's reasoning; I was really saying, "God, you blew it. You let me down. If I were you, I would do things differently." Suddenly I realized my error. Who was I to be so arrogant as to criticize and correct the omniscient Lord Almighty? But I also knew my grief and sorrow were very deep, and I asked myself, "What happens with that pain if I don't understand why?"

Two days later I read 2 Kings chapter 2, where the prophet Elijah is suddenly taken from his successor, Elisha, leaving Elisha in great sorrow. Verse 14 says that Elisha "struck the water with Elijah's cloak and cried out, 'Where is the LORD, the God of Elijah?' Then the river divided, and Elisha went across."

In my own sorrow I cried out, "Where now is the God of Elijah?" My heart was flooded with Scripture: "I am with you always" (Matt. 28:20). "A real friend sticks closer than a brother" (Prov. 18:24). "Can a mother forget her nursing child? . . . Even if that were possible, I would not forget you! See, I have written your name on the palms of my hands" (Isa. 49:15–16).

I didn't need to know why. It was enough to know that God was near.

— Andy Minch

My heart was flooded with Scripture: "I am with you always."

They do not fear bad news

they confidently

trust the Lord

to care for them

— PSALM 112:7

Do Not Fear

They do not fear bad news; they confidently trust the LORD to care for them.

— Psalm 112:7

A few years ago I was going through a difficult job situation. I was frustrated, confused, and angry. A friend suggested that I write down Scriptures and quotations that ministered to me. In my daily Bible reading it was hard to keep my mind on the Scriptures, as I was consumed with my problem. At night I tossed and turned, begging God to show me what he wanted me to do.

One evening I read Psalm 112, which I had read dozens of times before. But this time the words jumped off the page and spoke to my heart. I picked up my notebook and pen and copied the entire psalm. Before I put my head on my pillow, I memorized verse 7, "They [the righteous] do not fear bad news; they confidently trust the LORD to care for them."

Far from being angry and upset, I went to bed feeling hopeful and joyful.

I fell asleep immediately and slept soundly all night. Throughout that season of my life, whenever anger, confusion, or fear came knocking, I quoted this verse. It was my affirmation that not only should I trust the Lord to care for me, but I could trust him, because he is trustworthy.

As often happens, looking back now I see that God had a better plan for my future than I could have ever imagined.

Are you dealing with some bad news? Read and reflect on Psalm 112. Make verse 7 your prayer.

Praise the LORD!

How joyful are those who fear the LORD and delight in obeying his commands.

Their children will be successful everywhere; an entire generation of godly people will be blessed.

They themselves will be wealthy, and their good deeds will last forever.

Light shines in the darkness for the godly. They are generous, compassionate, and righteous.

Good comes to those who lend money generously and conduct their business fairly.

Such people will not be overcome by evil. Those who are righteous will be long remembered.

They do not fear bad news; they confidently trust the LORD to care for them.

They are confident and fearless and can face their foes triumphantly.

They share freely and give generously to those in need. Their good deeds will be remembered forever. They will have influence and honor.

The wicked will see this and be infuriated. They will grind their teeth in anger; they will slink away, their hopes thwarted.

— Julie Shimer

I HAVE
LOVED YOU
MY PEOPLE
WITH AN

EVERLASTING

Love

— JEREMIAH 31:3

An Everlasting Love

I have loved you, my people, with an everlasting love

— Jeremiah 31:3b

The national translators for the Mbam cluster of languages in Cameroon, West Africa, had gathered to say good-bye. I was leaving to spend an extended time at home in the United States.

I hadn't given a lot of thought to how I might encourage the translators to keep translating while I was gone. I decided to tell them a story about the Hdi people of Cameroon and how God had helped them recognize their word for unconditional love.

God prompted the project facilitator and translator, Lee, to ponder the Hdi word for love. Lee realized that he'd heard the Hdi people use two forms of the word—*dvi* and *dva*—but he'd never heard *dvu*, which the language patterns suggested should be possible.

I told the audience that Lee asked the Hdi translation committee, "Could you *dvi* your wife?" They said yes. *Dvi* meant that the wife had been loved in the past, but the love was gone.

I sensed that the Mbam speakers were tracking with me. They didn't have a grammar construction like that, but they knew what it meant to stop loving a wife.

I went on. Lee asked the Hdi men, "Could you *dva* your wife?" The Hdi men said yes. *Dva* love depended on the wife's actions, I explained. The wife would be loved as long as she remained faithful and cared for her husband well.

There were murmurs of agreement as the Mbam speakers acknowledged that, yes, they understood the meaning of *dva*. In their culture, too, wives were often treated like servants, receiving love as long as they were useful and faithful.

Then I repeated Lee's next question. "Could you *dvu* your wife?" To the Hdi men, that meant, "Could you love your wife even if she never got you water, or never made you meals? Even if she committed adultery—could you love her then?"

The Mbam speakers' response was immediate. They laughed—exactly as the Hdi translators had done when Lee asked them. It was clear that, like the Hdi men, they were thinking, "Of course not. That would never happen!"

Quietly, I quoted Lee's next words. "Could God *dvu* people?"

There was total silence. And then, one by one, these men who were responsible for conveying God's truths to their communities began to click their tongues, signaling their recognition of a surprising new truth. God loved them unconditionally. The idea was as new to them as it had been to the Hdi translators.

God loved them not because of what they did or how they loved him, but because it was in his divine nature to love them. He would never stop, whether or not they loved him, whether or not they served him, whether or not they were faithful to him.

— Patricia Wilkendorf

You saw me
before I was born

Every day
of ——————
my
life

was recorded in
your book

— PSALM 139:16

Written in Your Book

You saw me before I was born. Every day of my life was recorded in your book. Every moment was laid out before a single day had passed.

— Psalm 139:16

I just loved Georginio the moment I first saw him in his bright blue poncho with the red border, a little hand-knitted hat pulled over his dark hair, and black rubber boots that made him look like a miniature farmer. He was maybe three years old and didn't understand a word of my Spanish. Although I couldn't speak his Quechua language, we became fast friends. His sparkling eyes drew me in, and his funny little nose invited a quick tickle.

I was a teacher for missionary kids in a one-room schoolhouse in the Central Andes of Peru. On summer break I traveled to Georginio's village farther north to spend a few weeks teaching the children of two families who were working on a Bible translation project there. The majesty of the mountains seen from their village, the beauty of the sunsets, and the open expression on Georginio's little face filled me with a sense of awe and made me wonder why God had allowed me to be the one in the middle of this incredible experience.

As I entered the sunlit classroom one morning, I found the answer in a Bible passage the students and I were memorizing. Psalm 139 is an incredible poem of praise, and that day the second part of verse 16 seemed to call out to me.

"Every day of my life was recorded in your book. Every moment was laid out before a single day had passed."

God, the author of my life, had already written this chapter. He decided long ago that these experiences would be mine. He carefully penned each page of my book, adding a paragraph on growth here, a lesson on praise there. And on one page he drew the picture of a little Quechua boy in a blue poncho and black boots, with eyes that will forever smile in my memory, reminding me that God wrote Georginio's book too. And also reminding me that it is my privilege and yours to assist those who are working diligently to put another book—one with words of eternal life—into a language that will reach Georginio's heart.

Take a quiet moment to read Psalm 139 and think about the pages that God has written into your book. Have they been awe-inspiring and filled with joy? God wrote those experiences especially for you. Were you only too grateful to turn the page on a chapter of pain? In his wisdom, God penned those words for you. Thank him for being the author of your life!

— Rachel Yanac

The old life is
gone

a new life has

BEGUN!

— 2 CORINTHIANS 5:17

All Scripture Points to Christ

Anyone who belongs to Christ has become a new person. The old life is gone; a new life has begun!

— 2 Corinthians 5:17

When a young man named Demas showed up for an oral Bible storytelling workshop in Sandaun Province, Papua New Guinea, he seemed a little rough around the edges. He didn't know much about the Bible, but he was willing to learn.

Many people who don't have access to Scripture in their language are oral communicators—part of communities with no written language who pass down stories and information through storytelling. Demas is part of one such oral community.

At the workshop he studied stories from Genesis. Working with five others who spoke his language, Demas translated the stories and learned to tell them effectively. Each one of the stories taught him more about God's character and the way he relates to people. All Scripture points to Christ, and one evening toward the end of the course, Demas asked Jesus into his life.

Four months later, Demas came back for another workshop. Staff members hardly recognized him. His appearance had changed, and his face was radiant.

He said that shortly after he got home, his brother became ill and felt oppressed by an evil spirit. Family members asked the village's traditional healers to use their spells, charms, and chants to remove the spirit, but nothing helped. Demas offered to pray for his brother—but only if the family would stop asking for help from the healers and confess all the wrong things they'd done. The family accepted his offer and confessed their sins.

Demas prayed, and just a few hours later his brother felt the evil spirit leave him, and he returned to normal.

Demas told everyone the Bible stories he'd learned. Spiritual interest began to stir, and the once-dead church was revived! The villagers asked Demas to share devotions on Sundays. They constructed a church building and asked Demas to be the pastor. As God's Word in story form began to change lives, five young men felt led to enroll in Bible school.

Demas gave his report to the workshop participants with excitement, but quickly voiced a multitude of questions. What does it mean to be a pastor? Can I pray with someone to help them receive Christ? Can I baptize them? How do I deal with the traditional beliefs that keep my people in bondage?

A strong team of missionaries and Papua New Guinean trainers walked with Demas through Scripture and found answers to his questions. At the end of the workshop Demas went home stronger in the Lord, with more stories from God's Word to share and a deeper understanding of how to lead his people toward God.

Second Corinthians 5:17–18 says, "Anyone who belongs to Christ has become a new person. The old life is gone; a new life has begun! . . . And God has given us this task of reconciling people to him." Through engaging with God's Word, Demas experienced the life transformation that Jesus brings. By passing on what he learned, he reconciled others to God.

This is the lifestyle to which God has called each of us. My prayer is that we may be quick to learn, careful to respond, and faithful to pass on the story of his redeeming love.

— Carol Schatz

Wonderful
COUNSELOR

Mighty
GOD

Everlasting
FATHER

PRINCE OF
Peace

— ISAIAH 9:6-7

Peace Child

For a child is born to us, a son is given to us. The government will rest on his shoulders. And he will be called: Wonderful Counselor, Mighty God, Everlasting Father, Prince of Peace. His government and its peace will never end.

— Isaiah 9:6–7a

When my wife, Carol, and I settled among the Sawi people in what is today Papua, Indonesia, we dedicated ourselves to learning their unwritten language and working with them to translate the New Testament. Using methods taught to us by gifted Wycliffe instructors, we worked with the Sawi people, who soon had an alphabet.

All the while, enmity and open conflict existed between two Sawi villages that kept growing in ferocity with no police to intervene. Ultimately they reached a lasting peace—but only at great cost!

A father on one side of the conflict gave his only son to a father in the village of his enemies. As long as that baby boy—called a "peace child"—remained alive, the peace would be secure. And it was secure! All this, of course, prompted me to proclaim Jesus, God's only Son, as the ultimate peace child given by the greatest Father to secure eternal peace with God. But that was only the beginning.

With peace between those two newly reconciled villages, I began making a deeper penetration into the Sawi language. I found that the phrase I thought meant "forgive" actually means to "tolerate," as when someone is obnoxious! *Mar kedon*, "to heal the relationship," surfaced as a more clear and accurate way to say "forgive."

Eventually I asked if the peace child could ever be given back to his birth parents, and their answer was yes! After a few years, if people agreed by consensus that mutual respect was deeply instilled at last, the peace child could be consecrated back to his birth parents in a ceremony called *sasawadon*.

In *sasawadon*, what is consecrated to the birth parents is something that originally came from them. That is the meaning of "consecration" in God's Word! What can we possibly give to God that he has not already given to us?

— Don Richardson

What can we possibly give to God that he has not already given to us?

LET GOD
TRANSFORM YOU
INTO A *new* PERSON
BY CHANGING THE WAY
YOU
THINK

— ROMANS 12:2

Guided by the Bible

Don't copy the behavior and customs of this world, but let God transform you into a new person by changing the way you think. Then you will learn to know God's will for you, which is good and pleasing and perfect.

— Romans 12:2

I was raised without any religious instruction or experience, and I lived in numerous foster homes and orphanages. Throughout this time I developed intense anger, bordering on hate.

I was given a Bible at my high school graduation, which I disregarded, but which I somehow kept through college. I have always been an avid reader, and after college this Bible emerged as something I needed to check off my reading list. I decided to read it and get it out of the way. I read it like a textbook and became convinced that Jesus Christ is real! One night I gave my life to him and was astonished to find myself free of hatred, terror of dying, and acute claustrophobia—all issues I'd struggled with for years.

I was already married at the time, and we had started a family, yet I had no examples of healthy fathers or husbands to follow. My only experiences included parents fighting, divorcing, drinking, etc. So I set out to use the Bible to totally restructure my life and values. I used a dictionary to get the definitions of various words in the Bible so I would not be guessing about what the translators meant by choosing the words they did.

It has been almost sixty years now, and I am still walking in the faith and using the Bible as my source for life decisions and final truth. Romans 12:2 is a key verse for me, "Don't copy the behavior and customs of this world, but let God transform you into a new person by changing the way you think." Paul says that by doing this, we'll be able to discern what God's will is—what is good, pleasing, and perfect.

Through my personal experience and in learning about the high rate of illiteracy in the world, I have become driven to get God's Word to every person in a form they can use. The tremendous work of Wycliffe Bible Translators combined with Faith Comes By Hearing's recording of their work in audio has had a powerful impact on language groups as they read and listen to the truth. There are testimonies of transformed lives and positive changes, even in cultural traditions that had historically required things like vengeance, female mutilation, or drunkenness.

I am deeply grateful for the sacrifices that translators have made in an effort to give every person the opportunity to have the Bible in a language and form they can clearly understand. There is still a lot to do, but there is an army of people all over the world who are ready and willing to get the Bible into every language that needs it.

— Jerry Jackson

FOR I WAS HUNGRY

and you fed me

I WAS THIRSTY

and you gave me a drink

I WAS A STRANGER

and you invited me into your home

I WAS NAKED

and you gave me clothing

I WAS SICK

and you cared for me

I WAS IN PRISON

and you visited me

WHEN YOU DID IT TO ONE OF THE LEAST
OF THESE MY BROTHERS AND SISTERS
YOU WERE DOING IT TO ME!

— MATTHEW 25:35–36, 40

God's Economy

For I was hungry, and you fed me. I was thirsty, and you gave me a drink. I was a stranger, and you invited me into your home. I was naked, and you gave me clothing. I was sick, and you cared for me. I was in prison, and you visited me. . . . When you did it to one of the least of these my brothers and sisters, you were doing it to me!

— Matthew 25:35–36, 40

As missionaries with Wycliffe Bible Translators, we lived in Cameroon in western Africa for about eight years. We never truly understood our new environment in that time, but we grew to accept and enjoy many parts of it.

For example, it was never culturally improper for someone to ask for something, but we soon discovered it was a big "sin" to refuse to help. It was perceived as selfish. Helping could have meant offering someone food or clothing; it might also have meant listening, empathizing, inviting someone into our home, and extending friendship.

One thing we never completely felt comfortable with was the economic disparity between us expatriates and some of our Cameroonian friends. Bigger still was the disparity with beggars on the street. We simply had more financial resources than the vast majority of the people around us. But whatever theology I may have brought with me to Cameroon that said God's blessing is equated with money was completely eradicated in that culture. There we saw clearly how God's economy extends far beyond material resources.

In his Sermon on the Mount, Jesus said that God blesses those who are poor and realize their need for him. He blesses those who mourn, who are humble, who hunger and thirst for justice, and whose hearts are pure (Matt. 5:3–8).

Many believe the beatitudes Jesus preached in the Sermon on the Mount are largely patterned after the words of Isaiah 61:

"The Spirit of the Sovereign Lord is upon me, for the Lord has anointed me to bring good news to the poor. He has sent me to comfort the brokenhearted and to proclaim that captives will be released and prisoners will be freed. He has sent me to tell those who mourn that the time of the Lord's favor has come" (Isa. 61:1–2a).

Good news for the poor? God blesses those who are poor? That's what Jesus said. Sometimes it can be easier for someone without many resources to trust him fully. They realize their need for him. The kingdom of heaven is theirs.

This is the Good News Jesus delivered! In God's economy there is justice for all, and out of many peoples, races, religions, languages, and ancestries there is no longer Jew or Gentile, slave or free. We are all one in Christ Jesus.

— Bob Creson

HOLD FIRMLY

TO THE WORD OF

life

— PHILIPPIANS 2:16

Whining and Walking in Wokien

Do everything without complaining and arguing, so that no one can criticize you. Live clean, innocent lives as children of God, shining like bright lights in a world full of crooked and perverse people. Hold firmly to the word of life.

— Philippians 2:14–16a

It was the end of a long dry season in Papua New Guinea's Sepik region, and rain was scarce. We boiled river water to drink, but we were often so thirsty that we drank it still hot and full of silt. Our baby daughter, Brianna, was covered with more than three hundred bug bites. She had quit walking and sleeping through the night when we arrived in Wokien village for a short-term assignment. The list of our discomforts was long. We were hot, tired, and miserable.

I needed God!

I told God I'd listen if he kept me awake long enough to hear him. He did.

"Do everything without complaining and arguing, so that no one can criticize you. Live clean, innocent lives as children of God, shining like bright lights in a world full of crooked and perverse people. Hold firmly to the word of life" (Phil. 2:14–16a).

"Bonnie," I heard him say, "you're arguing with me that I'm not doing this right. I want your holiness before I want your service. What you see as hindrances are my tools to make you useful. Don't fight what I'm doing in you."

I surrendered to God, who knew better than me what he was doing.

The day before we hiked out of Wokien, we took one last walk through the village. My husband, John, set Brianna down and held out his fingers for her to grab while she tried to walk. After a few steps she let go and walked on her own! First twenty steps, then forty, then all the way back to the house.

God never changed our circumstances. But we let go of what we thought we needed in order to serve him in Papua New Guinea, and walked out of that village with a renewed relationship with the God of Grace.

— Bonnie Nystrom

> God never changed our circumstances. But we let go of what we thought we needed in order to serve him.

YOUR

presence
AMONG US

SETS YOUR PEOPLE AND ME APART
FROM ALL OTHER PEOPLE
ON THE EARTH

— EXODUS 33:16

The Presence of God

The LORD replied, "I will personally go with you, Moses, and I will give you rest—everything will be fine for you." Then Moses said, ". . . Your presence among us sets your people and me apart from all other people on the earth."

— Exodus 33:14–15a, 16b

The day dawned bright and clear on the eastern plains of Colombia with no hint of the surprises the day would hold. A military helicopter arrived at our mission center with a government investigative team and a contingent of navy frogmen. There had been false rumors that we were hiding a uranium mine at our center.

After careful inspections of our center, the commanding general led an intensive interrogation session. In late afternoon, the helicopter returned to the capital city. The frogmen, however, stayed for another ten days, carefully checking the nearby lake with special equipment for detecting radioactive ore.

During their stay, their commander had a birthday. We invited him and his men to a special birthday dinner in our home. My wife, Margaret, made the celebration complete with a cake in the shape of a navy ship with a tiny Colombian flag. We read to them from the Bible and gave each person a copy.

Before their departure, the commander met with me privately to apologize for the inconvenience they had caused. I assured him that we were happy they had come to learn the true nature of our work. In a surprising statement, he told me they had discovered only one thing during their investigation. I wondered if they had uncovered something suspicious.

Then to my great relief and joy, he said, "We found here the presence of God."

That's what the Christian life is all about—bringing into the presence of our Savior people who have never experienced his joy or his peace. What a privilege we have!

Lord, help me today, led by your Spirit, to manifest your presence to everyone I meet.

In Jesus's precious name,

Amen.

— Forrest Zander

> *To my great relief and joy, he said, "We found here the presence of God."*

My flesh
and my heart
may fail

–but–

GOD

–is the–

STRENGTH

of my heart

and my portion
forever

— PSALM 73:26 (NIV)

A Strong Heart

My flesh and my heart may fail, but God is the strength of my heart and my portion forever

— *Psalm 73:26 (NIV)*

Should we call 911? The pain in Martha's chest was not going away. It just kept getting worse and worse. So I called. Within minutes the ambulance was at our house taking her to the hospital.

When I found her in the emergency room, she said, "Did they tell you what's happening? I'm having a heart attack." I couldn't believe it. Martha was just thirty-four and had given birth to our third child less than three months earlier. After angioplasty and two stents, the doctor had saved her life, but there was significant damage resulting in heart failure. We were told that if her heart didn't improve over the next six months, she would need to have a defibrillator implanted to ensure that her heart would not stop beating unexpectedly one day.

Just two months prior we had made the decision to become missionaries with Wycliffe Bible Translators, committed to a life of helping people gain access to Scripture in a language they can clearly understand. But now we thought we would have to give up that dream. When Martha came home from the hospital, she opened her Bible to the book of Psalms, and the very first verse her eyes fixed upon was Psalm 73:26, "My flesh and my heart may fail, but God is the strength of my heart and my portion forever" (NIV).

Martha's heart had failed. But we trusted that God had a plan and would give us the strength we needed.

After much prayer, we felt the Lord telling us not to give up on our dream of joining Wycliffe. So we moved forward and spent the summer studying and preparing for our new career. Eight months later, we found out that Martha's heart had improved dramatically and that we were now approved to serve in Papua New Guinea.

Whenever we face difficult situations and obstacles, we know that God is our strength. We need not fear, because God is our portion and our inheritance. No matter what happens to us on earth, we know that we will be with the Lord forever. As long as we are in this world, God will give us the strength we need to accomplish his purposes.

— Adam Boyd

We need not fear, because God is our portion and our inheritance.

FOR THE **WORD** OF GOD IS

alive

&

POW

ERFUL

— HEBREWS 4:12

Dull Scissors and Sharp Swords

For the word of God is alive and powerful. It is sharper than the sharpest two-edged sword, cutting between soul and spirit, between joint and marrow. It exposes our innermost thoughts and desires.

— Hebrews 4:12

Several of us were sitting under a large veranda fabricated from bamboo and palm branches in the Democratic Republic of the Congo. Today was the celebration service for the translated book of Acts in the Mayogo language. I was prepared to speak if asked, although I wasn't looking forward to it. I don't like speaking to ten people in English, let alone speaking to a thousand in French!

As we started the dedication portion of the service, all I was asked to do was to cut the ribbon that surrounded the boxes, hold up a copy of Acts, and hand it to the pastor.

"I can do this," I thought. But I immediately knew I was in trouble when I picked up the scissors and the handle broke off. I was relieved to see that there was a tiny piece of metal to grip. I started to cut the ribbon but quickly made a second, more distressing discovery. I was holding not only the cheapest scissors in the country, but also the dullest. I might as well have tried to cut through titanium.

Great! Now a thousand people were staring at me. I persisted and finally cut through the ribbon. I opened a box, grasped one of the copies of Acts, and held it up for all to see. Then it hit me. I was holding in my hands the most powerful book ever written.

The next thought overwhelmed me like a flood. The message I had prepared was on Hebrews 4:12, "For the word of God is alive and powerful. It is sharper than the sharpest two-edged sword, cutting between soul and spirit, between joint and marrow. It exposes our innermost thoughts and desires." My weakness, and that of a dull pair of scissors, became more acute when I considered that the Word I held in the air that day was sharp enough to cut to their hearts, and mine.

Jesus said that he will build his church, and his powerful Word is a key ingredient. And—feeble vessels that we are—so are we.

Dull scissors and sharp swords. God is using them both to advance his kingdom.

— Jon Hampshire

> *Jesus said that he will build his church, and his powerful Word is a key ingredient.*

JESUS SENT HIM HOME SAYING TELL THEM EVERYTHING *God* HAS DONE FOR *you*

— LUKE 8:38-39

I'm Free

But Jesus sent him home, saying, "No, go back to your family, and tell them everything God has done for you." So he went all through the town proclaiming the great things Jesus had done for him.

— Luke 8:38b–39

Silence reigned in the room in southern Mexico where Fortunato, a Chamula speaker and Bible translator, was praying with the translation team. They'd just finished revising Luke 8:26–39, in which Jesus healed a demon-possessed man living in a village cemetery. Jesus worked on the fringes of society to include people who had previously been excluded, and this was a vivid picture of exclusion.

In his earlier years, before he trusted in Christ, Fortunato lived under the control of the gods of the Chamula and the powerful shamans who served them. He related very quickly to this story of healing. Just like the demon-possessed man, Fortunato's life had been filled with stormy restlessness. Just as Jesus had freed the man in the Bible, Fortunato had also been freed. Once excluded, now he was included! He was free!

Fortunato's tears came, and the room was filled with the sound of his muffled sobs, which turned into uncontrolled weeping. When he had regained control of his emotions enough to speak, Fortunato respectfully began to talk to God.

"Oh Lord, how well you remember how I, too, used to ask in my heart, 'Where, oh where, is there help?' And there was no help—only the harsh, unsatisfying counsel of the shamans. But how well you remember, Lord, when your wonderful help came. I have no way to pay you, but at least I can tell you over and over, 'Thank you, thank you, thank you!' And now, help us to get your wonderful message of help to all of my people. Amen."

Ken Jacobs, the Wycliffe translator working with the Chamula, remembers the day. "A long, respectful silence settled over those of us who waited with bowed heads," he said. "In some measure each of us shared the former private torment and the present overwhelming relief of modern-day men . . . whom Jesus had touched with his Word."

— Carol Schatz

> "Oh Lord, how well you remember how I, too, used to ask in my heart, 'Where, oh where, is there help?'"

For a fuller account of Fortunato's story, read These Words Changed Everything *by David Aeilt.*

Faith

is the evidence of things we

cannot see

— HEBREWS 11:1

Losing Feathers

Faith shows the reality of what we hope for; it is the evidence of things we cannot see.

— Hebrews 11:1

I remember the time back on our family chicken farm when Dad, for economic reasons, decided to molt our old flock of chickens instead of selling them off and buying a new flock. Withholding food from the chickens for a few days forced them into a molt where they began to lose their feathers en masse.

In every corner of the chicken house, mounds of recently shed feathers swirled around. While waiting for new feathers to grow out, the bare-skinned chickens without wing feathers could no longer fly up to roost in high places as they were used to doing.

This memory returned to me during my last trip to Nigeria for a translation workshop on James. During this workshop, we discussed how to translate the word *faith* in verses like James 2:26, which says, "Faith is dead without good works." Many of the twenty language teams at the workshop used a phrase that was borrowed from Hausa—the trade language in that area of Nigeria—and translated literally into their language. Some of us questioned whether this was the best way to translate *faith*, so as a group we looked for other solutions.

One translator from a language to the south shared that his language had an idiom for faith. This idiom is literally "lose feathers." What does losing feathers have to do with faith? He explained that there is a species of bird in his area that, upon hatching its eggs, loses its feathers. During this molting phase, the mother bird is no longer able to fly away from the nest and look for food for her hungry hatchlings. She has to remain in the nest where she and her babies are completely dependent upon the male bird to bring them food. Without the diligent, dependable work of the male bird, the mother and babies would all die. This scenario was the basis for the word for *faith* in his language.

What a beautiful picture of faith and trust. We humans in our sinful condition are unable to save ourselves. Except for the work of the Lord, we would all die. But he is completely trustworthy. As we put our trust in him and depend on him, he provides for our needs both now and in the life to come.

— Randy Groff

We humans in our sinful condition are unable to save ourselves.

I WILL **RESCUE** THOSE WHO
LOVE ME
I WILL **PROTECT** THOSE WHO
TRUST
IN MY NAME

— PSALM 91:14

A Flat Tire

For he will order his angels to protect you wherever you go. They will hold you up with their hands so you won't even hurt your foot on a stone. You will trample upon lions and cobras; you will crush fierce lions and serpents under your feet! The LORD says, "I will rescue those who love me. I will protect those who trust in my name."

— Psalm 91:11–14

As soon as night had fallen, one of our car tires went flat. We'd been in Papua New Guinea only a few months, but we'd heard many times that holdups on the roads were not uncommon at night. In spite of efforts to leave sooner, we found that our 3:30 p.m. departure from the highlands for an appointment in the coastal city of Madang meant that we would still be on the road an hour after the sun had set.

As I sat in the backseat of our sedan with our one-year-old daughter and newborn son in what seemed like the middle of nowhere, my husband, Jerry, pulled out the spare tire and began to loosen the lug nuts on the flat one. Peering out at the dark jungle on either side of us and then at the road ahead, I felt my body tense as I watched the headlights of an approaching vehicle.

The pickup truck stopped near our car, and my heart pounded as several men jumped down from the truck and surrounded the back of our car. No sooner had I called out to God to help and protect us than I felt the car being lifted off the ground with my children and me still sitting inside. Desperately I continued to pray that we would not be harmed. Hardly a minute later, the men set the car back down, climbed back into their truck, and took off.

These men had joined together to become a human car jack allowing Jerry to swiftly change the tire so we could be on the move again!

We have no idea who those men were. For all we know, they could even have been angels. But one thing we do know— we serve a great and mighty God. He rescues and protects those who trust his name (Ps. 91:14).

When have you experienced the Lord's protection?

— Sue Pfaff

> We serve a great and mighty God. He rescues and protects those who trust in his name.

Jesus got up
and went out to
an isolated place

to pray

Refueling Doers

Before daybreak the next morning, Jesus got up and went out to an isolated place to pray.

— Mark 1:35

When Jeanette and I first started dating, one of our favorite television commercials was for Energizer batteries. We loved the little pink Energizer Bunny and his drum. The slogan was like a mantra for our generation: "He keeps going and going and going . . ."

We're extroverts! We love being around people and doing stuff. When we took the Myers-Briggs personality test, our "E" scores for extrovert were so far off the charts that we couldn't see the "I" for introvert. On more than one occasion we've been told, "You two are a ball of energy!" People like us can be a whole lot coming at you. Our passion and gratitude for what we've been given can cause us to go, go, go.

The Jesus of Mark's Gospel—we call him "Action Jesus"—is very appealing for us active types. In Mark, Jesus is a man of action followed by crowds. The allure of busyness and crowds is powerful in a world of demands like ours. There's nothing wrong with being active and being around people. Much of Scripture is filled with commands to go, preach, teach, and heal. Still, doers can't go on forever without life-giving replenishment.

One night in Raleigh, North Carolina, the secret strength of "Action Jesus" became very real to us. Our sermon title that evening was "Fire in Our Bones!" Yet, ironically, all we felt when we returned to our hotel room was sheer exhaustion. We were in the middle of a project for refugee children that had hit a snag, and despite a great night of worship, we were running on empty.

It was here, at almost midnight in a hotel room in North Carolina, that God's Word breathed anew on us. We heard the secret of Jesus's action in the heart of the Gospel of Mark: "Jesus went out to an isolated place to pray" (Mark 1:35). We are still doers, but we recalibrate. We are continually challenged to be fueled, grounded, and recharged in the abiding presence of God and his Word.

Have you too been drawn away from the refreshing presence of God and the nourishment of his Word? Perhaps you are action people like us (and that's okay!). But listen to God inviting you anew, "Come be with me and find rest and fuel for your soul!"

— Gabriel and Jeanette Salguero

> **Doers can't go on forever without life-giving replenishment.**

SO THE
Word
BECAME
HUMAN
AND MADE HIS HOME AMONG
US

— JOHN 1:14

Life-Changing News

So the Word became human and made his home among us. He was full of unfailing love and faithfulness. And we have seen his glory, the glory of the Father's one and only Son.

— John 1:14

When my wife, Dallas, and I moved to Cameroon, we made friends quickly. Two of our closest friends were Léonard and Marie Bolioki. Léo understood the deep impact of the translated Word long before Dallas and I arrived in Cameroon. He tells this story about a Good Friday service in his church:

I stepped to the front of the church and began to read the story of Jesus's crucifixion. Always before, this passage from John's Gospel had been read in French, but this time I was asked to read it in my own language, Yambetta.

As I read, I became aware of a growing stillness. Then some of the older women began to weep. At the end of the service, they rushed up to me and asked, "Where did you find this story? We have never heard anything like it before! We didn't know there was someone who loved us so much that he was willing to suffer and die like that—to be crucified on a cross to save us!"

I pulled out my French New Testament and showed them the passage in the Gospel of John and said, "We listen to this story every year during Holy Week." But they insisted that they'd never heard it before. That is what motivated me to translate the Scriptures into the only language my friends and family can really understand—Yambetta!

Jesus came into the world with the intention of moving in among us. John's Gospel says, "So the Word became human and made his home among us. He was full of unfailing love and faithfulness. And we have seen his glory, the glory of the Father's one and only Son" (John 1:14).

Revelation 3:20 says that Jesus is standing at the door, knocking and speaking in a voice people can understand. "If you hear my voice and open the door, I will come in, and we will share a meal together as friends," he says.

"Open the door! I want to come into your lives." This is the message Léonard's community understood the day he read the Yambetta Scriptures in church.

Chris Webb puts it this way in his book *The Fire of the Word:* "This ancient book has spoken into my contemporary world with startling clarity and irresistible authority. . . . The presence of God breaks into this world and bursts with unpredictable consequences into our lives. . . . The Bible clearly has the potential to provoke the most radical and far-reaching changes in individuals, societies and nations."

This is life-changing news—God's eternal Word that informs and transforms all of life!

— Bob Creson

AND THE GOOD NEWS ABOUT THE KINGDOM

WILL BE

Preached

THROUGHOUT THE

W H O L E

WORLD

SO THAT

ALL NATIONS WILL HEAR IT

AND THEN
THE END WILL COME

— MATTHEW 24:14

The Great Message

And the Good News about the Kingdom will be preached throughout the whole world, so that all nations will hear it; and then the end will come.

— Matthew 24:14

I was thinking today about what you would read if you were to get out a file of newspapers from the last fifty years and see what the world has called the significant events during that time.

What if you were reading God's record of events that have occurred during the last fifty years? I'm sure that it would be quite different from what the world considers to be important. I have no doubt in the annals of heaven that one of the most significant events of the last half-century has been the explosion of Bible translation, which has brought the Word of God to hundreds of tribes and languages.

Much of this is because of the vision and genius of Cameron Townsend, founder of Wycliffe Bible Translators. He was a university dropout, with an urgent desire to serve the Lord wherever the Lord should lead him. And this should encourage many of you—that the thing about going into this type of ministry is that God can take a dedicated heart and consecrate it to his service and shake the world.

You have to face squarely if your talents, and your gifts, and your training prepare you for Christian service. In fact it might be said that Jesus only had two verbs: *come* and *go*. "Come unto me," and, "Go into all the world."

Go out quickly into the streets and into the lanes. Go out into the highways and hedges. Go into the vineyard. Go into the village. Go into the city. Go into the town. Go to the lost sheep. Go thou and preach the kingdom of God. Go ye into all the world!

If you profess the name of the Lord Jesus Christ, you have that command and you have to face it. You have to do something about it.

Consider the message that we have to proclaim! The early apostles had no doubt about their message, and neither did Cameron Townsend.

This is a serious, critical hour in the history of the world, but it's also a great hour for the gospel, because we're the only ones who have the message of hope. We know what the future holds. God has the future planned. And we have a responsibility to see that every language has the Word of God written in it.

— Billy Graham

Jesus only had two verbs: come and go. "Come unto me," and, "Go into all the world."

This message was originally part of Billy Graham's sermon at Wycliffe's Jubilee service at the Anaheim Convention Center in 1981, celebrating fifty years since Cameron Townsend completed the Cakchiquel New Testament translation.

I can never escape from your Spirit!
I can never get away from your presence!

**IF I GO UP TO HEAVEN
YOU ARE THERE**

**IF I GO DOWN TO THE GRAVE
YOU ARE THERE**

— PSALM 139:7-8

Who's Holding the Rope?

I can never escape from your Spirit! I can never get away from your presence! If I go up to heaven, you are there; if I go down to the grave, you are there. If I ride the wings of the morning, if I dwell by the farthest oceans, even there your hand will guide me, and your strength will support me.

— Psalm 139:7–10

Once in Oaxaca, Mexico, I led a story time for missionary children about trust. I shared about the man who was hired to climb down one of our wells to clean it out. Two other men tied a rope around him and lowered him into the forty-foot hole. The well cleaner then scooped slush, sand, and rocks with a shovel, filling bucket after bucket to be hauled up with the rope.

I told the children to imagine themselves being lowered into that deep, dark hole, and I asked them what kind of person they'd want at the other end of the rope. One child said, "Somebody strong," and we all agreed it should be someone who could pull you back out of the hole.

Another child said, "Somebody who wouldn't walk away," and we agreed the rope holder should be someone responsible who wouldn't get distracted and forget you down there.

We also didn't want someone who might play a practical joke on you; it should be somebody who cared about you and had your best interest in mind.

I then asked, "If you were going to have somebody with all these qualities hold the rope for you while you were in the well, who would you pick?"

"I'd pick my dad," one girl said with confidence.

There were no arguments that a dad would be a good choice. A dad is strong. A dad loves you, is responsible and dependable, and wouldn't leave you by yourself. A dad is faithful. A dad has your best interest in mind. At that point, one of the children added, "And a dad would never play tricks on you when you were in the well."

I asked if they could think of anyone else with "dad" qualities. Right on cue, someone piped up, "God!"

Going through life, we sometimes find ourselves at the end of our rope. It is very comforting and reassuring to know who is hanging on to the other end—someone strong, faithful, and dependable, who cares about you and loves you.

— Carol Sissel

> *It is very comforting and reassuring to know who is hanging on to the other end.*

FOR WE ARE

God's

masterpiece HE HAS **CREATED**

US ANEW

in **CHRIST JESUS**

Created Anew

For we are God's masterpiece. He has created us anew in Christ Jesus, so we can do the good things he planned for us long ago.

— Ephesians 2:10

I grew up in a home that honored Christ. We always ate together as a family, with Bible reading and prayer at the table each morning and evening. I remember memorizing and quoting Scriptures. When I was ten, my father told me that if I read three chapters of the Bible every weekday and five on Sunday, I could read through the entire Bible in exactly a year. So I did it, to see if it worked out that neatly. And it did! Some things in Scripture I didn't understand, and other parts seemed strange, but I enjoyed it and was fascinated by what I read.

My parents always made it clear that a commitment to follow Christ was a personal decision for me to make. I didn't make that commitment until my junior year in high school. I was a substitute on our school basketball team. That year we won the city finals by a free throw after the final whistle ended the overtime. The gymnasium became a madhouse, but the most exciting moment of my life seemed meaningless and empty. I remember asking God to show me what was wrong with me. And he did.

My father and I were invited for supper at the home where Dr. L. S. Chafer, a visiting Bible teacher, was staying. While we were chatting on the veranda waiting for the meal, Dr. Chafer quietly switched the conversation from another topic and asked me if I had ever personally accepted Christ as my Savior. I said, "No, I haven't."

"Well, don't you want to?" he responded in a surprised tone that implied I was missing the greatest thing in life. My heart was ready, and I said yes.

I wasn't prepared for the radical change that took place in me. Although I had read the Bible cover-to-cover six times (I was now sixteen) and had memorized many passages, it came alive in a new way. I remember how shocked I was to hear myself say, when I had to decide between two possible courses in my senior year, "I wonder which one the Lord would have me take?" I had never asked myself that question before. Then it dawned on me that Christ was Lord, and I was under new management!

Thinking ahead to college and choosing a career were major concerns. Then I read Ephesians 2:10 and realized God had the good works he wanted me to do already planned. It wasn't my decision to make; he had already made it! My responsibility was to live into the future he had planned.

But how? By letting him speak to me through my Bible reading, talking it over with him in prayer, and by watching for indications of his will in my circumstances and in the counsel of Christian friends.

He gave me so many opportunities, including the gift of being involved, along with my wife, Florence, in worldwide Bible translation. The Word of God transformed and informed my life!

— George Cowan

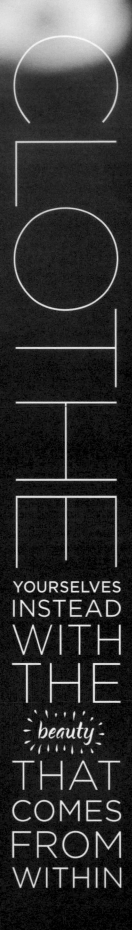

CLOTHE

YOURSELVES
INSTEAD
WITH
THE
beauty
THAT
COMES
FROM
WITHIN

— 1 PETER 3:4

Pretty as a Plum

Don't be concerned about the outward beauty of fancy hairstyles, expensive jewelry, or beautiful clothes. You should clothe yourselves instead with the beauty that comes from within.

— 1 Peter 3:3–4a

had not expected to see the word for "plum" right in the middle of 1 Peter 3:3, but there it was! When our team translated the verse from the Gunu language back into English, it read, "Wives, don't try to be pretty like a market plum, by braiding your hair and putting on gold jewelry and beautiful clothes." Concerned for clear, natural, and accurate Bible translation, I asked the Gunu translation team, "Why did you use that word?"

Their explanation made perfect sense. A favorite fruit in their area of Cameroon is the *safou*, or African plum. Sold in the local market, these plums look beautiful early in the day—all purple and shiny—and they taste great! But after a long day of sitting out in the warm African sun, although they still look pretty, the plums have lost their freshness and they taste terrible!

So "pretty like a market plum," for the Gunu people, is a metaphor for superficial beauty, and that's exactly what Peter was talking about in 1 Peter 3:3. English translations of that verse refer to "outward adornment" or "outward beauty."

"Don't be concerned about the outward beauty or fancy hairstyles, expensive jewelry, or beautiful clothes. You should clothe yourselves instead with the beauty that comes from within, the unfading beauty of a gentle and quiet spirit, which is so precious to God" (1 Pet. 3:3–4).

While the context is Peter writing to women, I hope we can also see a clear connection to men; let's not miss that! True inner beauty for men and women comes from what's on the inside—what's in our hearts—not from what's outside. If we have a gentle and quiet spirit, it will most likely be evident on the outside too. And as Peter says, this is precious to God.

We also see this principle elsewhere in the Scriptures. When Samuel was asked to select a king for Israel, he took one look at Eliab and thought, "Surely this is the LORD's anointed!" But the Lord said to Samuel, "Don't judge by his appearance. . . . The LORD doesn't see things the way you see them. People judge by outward appearance, but the LORD looks at the heart" (1 Sam. 16:6–7).

Jeremiah says the Lord searches our hearts and examines motives, giving rewards according to what our actions deserve (Jer. 17:10). And Jesus said, "The words you speak come from the heart—that's what defiles you" (Matt. 15:18).

Let's honor God and each other with our words and deeds. Make every effort not to be pretty like a market plum in the afternoon sun—pretty on the outside but bitter on the inside.

— Keith Patman

GIVE YOUR
BODIES TO

GOD

BECAUSE
OF ALL HE HAS
DONE FOR
YOU

ROMANS 12:1

Cumbersome Clothing

And so, dear brothers and sisters, I plead with you to give your bodies to God because of all he has done for you. Let them be a living and holy sacrifice—the kind he will find acceptable. This is truly the way to worship him.

— Romans 12:1

I still remember the day our family arrived by horseback in Colombia's Andes Mountains to a breathtaking panorama of Guambiano-land, which would become our home. We were confident that God would use us in his way to bring the gospel to this people group. We began looking for ways to gain their trust.

My husband, Tom, who had never planted a bean in his life, learned agriculture in the fields of Guambia, reading all he could get his hands on about planting potatoes, bringing in new seed, and using fertilizers and fumigation in hopes that better profits could be reaped from those rocky mountains. My outreach seemed limited as I cared for our young children, kept the house clean, put meals on the table, and cared for those few timid ones who stopped by our kitchen, which also served as a clinic, for medical help.

One day a Guambiano woman sat waiting patiently for medicine as I struggled with my attire—a heavy, hand-woven, wool pleated skirt tied on with a brightly colored belt to keep it from slipping down. It was so tight I could hardly breathe, but all the local women wore them.

I struggled with my elegant blue wool shawl, just like hers, the edges flapping through the remains of bowls of oatmeal as I cleaned off the kitchen counter. These clothes were more suited to her lifestyle—sitting on a log close to the floor over an open fire. But I was determined to identify with these people no matter what. Very quietly and respectfully, the woman issued a wake-up call as she murmured truth, "Señora, you will never be a Guambiano."

It was in that gentle rebuke that God spoke to my frustrations. My identity was to be in him! I was not called to be an American or a Guambiano, but to conform to his image. Only then would I be able to know his good, pleasing, and perfect will for me among the Guambianos.

Years later, I stood on the bank of an icy, rushing river to see Guambiano women being baptized. They were wearing their same cumbersome costumes but were released from the fear and bondage of their old beliefs. I could then indeed truly identify with them as sisters in the Lord, each of us saved by his grace and part of his glorious body.

— Judy Branks

It was in that gentle rebuke that God spoke to my frustrations.

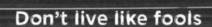

Don't live like fools

Make the most of

every

opportunity

in these evil days

EPHESIANS 5:15-16

God's Opportunities

So be careful how you live. Don't live like fools, but like those who are wise. Make the most of every opportunity in these evil days.

— Ephesians 5:15-16

It was 6:30 a.m. on a Saturday morning in Sioux Falls, South Dakota. I was checking out of my hotel room and had just enough time to catch a light breakfast at the hotel clubroom before I left for the airport.

The clubroom had just opened, and the only other person in the room was the woman who worked there. As I quickly ate my yogurt and granola, I learned that the woman, Mindy, was a single mom raising three teenagers. Her ex-husband was not contributing to their support, so she worked at a full-time job Monday through Friday and opened the clubroom Saturday and Sunday mornings. I learned she was a Christian but sensed she was stressed.

This was a wide-open door to touch a life in need. I gave Mindy a book on living life above everyday circumstances and asked if I could pray for her. She said yes, and I prayed for several minutes that God would meet Mindy's needs and give her peace.

When I looked at Mindy's face after we prayed, I saw tears streaming down her cheeks. God had touched her life.

Why did I take that time? I was running the risk of being late for my flight. Well, I have learned from God's Word that "we are God's masterpiece. He has

created us anew in Christ Jesus, so we can do the good things he planned for us long ago" (Eph. 2:10).

God had arranged for me to meet Mindy at a time of need and had prepared me to know how to minister to her. This was a God-given opportunity. I have also learned through the years that God expects me to notice and take advantage of the opportunities he provides. "So be careful how you live. . . . Make the most of every opportunity" (Eph. 5:15-16).

Because of what God's Word had taught me, it was clear that ministering to Mindy was something I needed to do. So I did.

Ask yourself, "Do I go through my day asking God to show me the special opportunities that he wants me to make the most of?" God's Word says we can expect them to come. Will we notice them and count them as interruptions to be avoided, or as blessings to be received?

— Steve Douglass

This was a wide-open door to touch a life in need.

FOR THE

DARKNESS

IS DISAPPEARING

AND THE

TRUE LIGHT

IS ALREADY SHINING

— 1 JOHN 2:8

Cleaning the Connections

This old commandment—to love one another—is the same message you heard before
Yet it is also new. Jesus lived the truth of this commandment, and you also are living it.
For the darkness is disappearing, and the true light is already shining.

— 1 John 2:7b–8

It was a dark and stormy night.

It really was! I've been laughed at for starting a story that way. But when you're piloting a vintage DC-3 airliner and trying to make an instrument landing on an island in the West Indies with your automatic direction finder (ADF) out of whack, and it's a dark and stormy night—what else can you say? I can assure you it was no laughing matter.

That night as I approached Kingston, Jamaica, in a screaming gale, my ADF chose to rebel. It pointed straight ahead for a while. Then it pointed over toward Spain. At one point it aimed to the rear. Fortunately, I had dual ADFs on the plane; the second one remained loyal, and I landed safely.

Later, I watched the radio repairman troubleshoot the faulty ADF. After a few simple clicks, he turned and said, "You'll never keep it on course with a bad connection, Captain. The problem is in this cannon plug."

I watched as he disassembled the complicated plug. Moisture in the connections had caused corrosion to build up. The unwanted resistance in the wires resulted in an unreliable ADF.

Besides getting an instrument repaired, I got some good advice. "Every so often, Captain," he remarked, "you need to stop and clean up your connections."

I was reminded of that phrase later when our family went on a vacation to the beach. There is nothing like five people in a crowded camper to test the condition of your wiring.

At the end of the first day it was apparent that we had some fragile connections. The best communication we could manage was a lot of harsh static. My wife threatened to go home. My oldest son, a high school senior, took courage in the fact that this would be his last family vacation. We couldn't even agree on what kind of soda pop to drink.

The next morning I decided we had to clean up some connections. We examined ourselves—each one in relation to the others. We found that parents aren't always fair and that resentments build up between brothers. We leveled with one another, confessed, prayed, cleaned up the connections, and went on to have one of our best family vacations ever.

Lesson learned. If I'm going to stay on course and be effective in my life and ministry, I'm going to have to keep the connections clean—because for sure, there will be more dark and stormy nights.

— Bernie May

FOR
CHRIST
DIED
TO SET THEM
FREE

— HEBREWS 9:15

Taking God Seriously

For by the power of the eternal Spirit, Christ offered himself to God as a perfect sacrifice for our sins. That is why he is the one who mediates a new covenant between God and people, so that all who are called can receive the eternal inheritance God has promised them. For Christ died to set them free from the penalty of the sins they had committed under that first covenant.

— Hebrews 9:14b–15

"My uncle's new God is no different from all the gods of our ancestors," Mariano grumbled. "He demands perfection just like they do, and I cannot attain it!"

Reading Scripture in his Chamula language for the first time, Mariano had come across Mark 9:43, "If your hand causes you to sin, cut it off. It's better to enter eternal life with only one hand than to go into the unquenchable fires of hell with two hands."

The Ten Commandments were no more encouraging. "I can't keep those laws!" he thought.

Mariano's people believed in a lower world full of bad spirits; so he could imagine hell. He also knew about sin. He'd tried and failed to rid his life of hate and jealousy and anger. He'd tried to measure up to the capricious demands of the Chamula gods of wood and stone, and to appease them through ritual drunkenness and animal sacrifices—again without success.

Deeply troubled, he agreed to work with a Wycliffe translator named Ken Jacobs to translate the Bible for his people. He soon discovered that he loved translation, and he was good at it!

They were most of the way through the book of Hebrews when Mariano understood for the first time that Jesus Christ was the perfect sacrifice for his sin. "I can hardly believe that what I'm hearing in the Bible is true!" he exclaimed. "The Good News is not an order like the demands that we've received from our Chamula gods. It's an offer! The sins that have kept all the people in the world from God are forgiven.

"Because of Jesus's sacrifice, God points to himself saying, 'Look, I make myself responsible to do for you what you cannot do for yourself.' He offers to govern our lives and help us live a life that is pleasing to him—to take us from where we are to where he wants us to go."

"If that is God's offer and you wanted to accept it, what would you say to him?" asked Ken.

Mariano's next words turned out to be the perfect way for a Chamula to express the concept of faith. "I would take seriously and hold in high esteem what God had obligated himself to do."

For several days Mariano wrestled with the implications of following Jesus. He knew he had not governed himself well, but he found it hard to give up control of his life.

Finally one morning he told Ken, "That's what I want!" He turned his life over to God, and peace filled his heart.

In the years that followed, Mariano helped others understand God's offer of forgiveness and grace. "I was an unbeliever who heard in my language that God had obligated himself to take care of my sins and to do for me what I could not do for myself," he said. "I took God seriously."

— Carol Schatz

For a fuller account of Mariano's story, read These Words Changed Everything *by David Aeilt.*

— BE —

thankful

IN ALL

CIRCUMSTANCES

— 1 THESSALONIANS 5:18

No Complaints

Be thankful in all circumstances, for this is God's will for you who belong to Christ Jesus.

— 1 Thessalonians 5:18

Every time I start to complain, I think of Paka's impressive decision not to.

The very lowliest member of a tiny group of Palikur Indians hidden in the Amazon jungle, Paka had Parkinson's disease for many years. He was constantly falling down. He splashed into the mud, or crashed into a firewood pile, or plunged into the fire itself. On top of this, his wife, Anudai, was born blind. They were the poorest of the poor. It is hard enough to survive in the jungle when you are strong and well. When you have a disability, it is almost impossible. But they are survivors.

Paka and Anudai shone with the joy of the Lord. From the time they first heard about him in 1969, they really loved him. The Lord was all they had, and he was enough. Paka was the first to arrive at every worship service, always ready to request his favorite hymn, "Fairest Lord Jesus." Though he could not read the Scriptures, he listened intently to every word and put them into practice.

Paka wanted to serve the Lord, but there was very little he could do. One day he heard that God's Word says to be thankful in all circumstances. He decided that every time he fell down, he would thank the Lord. From that time on thanksgiving became his automatic reaction to every tumble he took.

He would immediately call out, "Thank you, Lord, for being with me no matter what happens! Thank you for helping me get back up. Thank you that I can depend on you. Thank you for healing me. Thank you for loving me!"

That reaction made a deep impression on the other people in his village. If Paka could thank God in his situation, how could they complain about their problems?

Paka's decision to obey God in this one small area had a tremendous effect on all the people in his community—a greater effect than many eloquent sermons could have had. His simple obedience of that one little sentence literally changed his neighbors' minds and attitudes—and mine too!

— Diana Green

Thanksgiving became his automatic reaction to every tumble he took.

HOW I WISH TODAY THAT YOU OF

ALL PEOPLE WOULD UNDERSTAND

the way to

PEACE

— LUKE 19:42

The Least, Last, and Lost

But as he came closer to Jerusalem and saw the city ahead, he began to weep, "How I wish today that you of all people would understand the way to peace."

— Luke 19:41–42a

Wycliffe missionaries Amber and Terrill Schrock live in the mountains of northeastern Uganda, at the end of a dirt path that leads to a dirt road that leads to an airstrip. Some might say they live in the middle of nowhere.

Having visited there and read descriptions of the Ik people, who also live in this remote village, I understand why some might think they're unimportant. But that wouldn't be fair to the Ik. Numbering about ten thousand people, the Ik have been regularly raided by neighboring people groups. Colin Turnbull, a British anthropologist, wrote a book about the Ik in which he describes them as a people "beyond hope."

In Luke 12, the crowds following Jesus begin growing until thousands of people are milling about. They've come to hear him preach and to be healed of their diseases. Jesus appears to grow desperate for people to understand his message—to understand the heart of the Father. In chapter 13, verse 34, he says, "O Jerusalem, Jerusalem, the city that kills the prophets and stones God's messengers! How often I have wanted to gather your children together as a hen protects her chicks beneath her wings, but you wouldn't let me."

Then in Luke 15 he tells three stories about the depth of God's love: the Parable of the Lost Sheep, the Parable of the Lost Coin, and the Parable of the Lost Son. Each is a fabulous story of God's love. The lost sheep shows the extent God will go to for the one; the lost coin illustrates how finding God is the most important thing in the world.

My favorite story is the Parable of the Lost Son. Having squandered his inheritance, totally disgraced and living with the pigs in abject cultural abomination and rejection, the son returns home and the father reaches out to him. "While he was still a long way off, his father saw him coming. Filled with love and compassion, he ran to his son, embraced him, and kissed him" (Luke 15:20).

Grace. Most people understand it incorrectly, like this son did. "I am no longer worthy of being called your son," he said. He just hoped to be hired as his father's servant. There is nothing we can do to earn grace! It's God's free gift.

But the real story is the heart of the Father—the extent God will go to for us. This is grace. Is anyone or any community beyond hope? The Schrocks don't think so. They've experienced God's grace in their own lives, and they want to pass it on. That's why they've chosen to live at the end of that dirt path, believing that God decided in advance to adopt the Ik people into his own family, and he wanted to use the Schrocks to do it. The Schrocks have dedicated themselves to translating God's Word—his message of grace—for the Ik.

— Bob Creson

Come close to God

and

GOD

will come
close to you

— JAMES 4:8

We're All Beggars

Come close to God, and God will come close to you.

— James 4:8a

Being rich among the very poor is tough. My wife, Amber, and I work among the Ik people of northeastern Uganda, where we are often asked for goods and services. But as we have studied the language and culture, the Ik people have taught us some important things about God.

In the Ik language, the word *waan* means "beg."

It also means "pray."

What do begging and praying have to do with each other? Do you beg when you pray? Do I?

The Ik word for "visitor" is *waanam*, which means "begging person." Do you beg when you go visiting? The Ik do. Maybe you don't beg, but maybe when you visit someone, you are looking for something. Maybe it's just a listening ear.

When the Ik hear that Amber and I are planning a trip to this or that place for a certain amount of time, the letters and lists start coming. As the days dwindle before our departure, the little stack of requests grows. "Please, sir, remember me for the following: shoes, jacket (rainproof), watch, box, trousers, pens, and money for the children. Thank you, sir, for your assistance."

A few people come by just to greet us or spend a bit of time with us. Another precious few will occasionally confide in us about their problems without asking for anything more than a listening ear. I love that.

The other day I was in our spare bedroom praying my list of requests to God—a nice list covering most areas of my life, certainly all the points of anxiety. Then it hit me: Does God want my list, or does he want my relationship?

I decided to try something. Instead of reading off my list of requests to God, I just talk to him about my issues without any expectation of how he should respond. I make it more about our relationship than my list, because if our personhood is like God's personhood, then maybe God prefers our confidence and time to our lists, letters, and enumerations.

— Terrill Schrock

Instead of reading off my list of requests to God, I just talk to him about my issues without any expectation of how he should respond.

HE WENT

WITHOUT

KNOWING

WHERE HE
WAS GOING

HEBREWS 11:8

In Abraham's Footsteps

It was by faith that Abraham obeyed when God called him to leave home and go to another land that God would give him as his inheritance. He went without knowing where he was going. And even when he reached the land God promised him, he lived there by faith—for he was like a foreigner.

— Hebrews 11:8–9a

If Bible translators were to have a "patron saint," I think it would be Abraham. In the book of Genesis, beginning with chapter 12, we read how God called him out of the land where he was living and led him to another land.

Hebrews 11:8–10 gives us special insights about Abraham. It says he obeyed and went, even though he did not know where he was going. Then he lived as a foreigner in the land that God called him to and promised to him. It didn't bother him that he lived in tents, because he "was confidently looking forward to a city with eternal foundations, a city designed and built by God."

Like Abraham, my husband and I responded to God's call and went to a place that we were unfamiliar with. We went as Bible translators to Brazil and began work with the Wayampi people.

Over time we have been changed by our experiences with both Brazilian nationals and the Wayampi. Both these cultures place a high value on community, and we learned from them to pay more attention to personal relationships. From them we learned to live more simply, and we learned to see our home country through their eyes. But despite the adjustments we made, we are always aware of the fact that we are neither Brazilian nor Wayampi; we never will be. There are aspects of both cultures that will always be a struggle for us.

That didn't really surprise us, but what did take us by surprise on our first furlough was the discovery that we were no longer completely at home in our own country either. It wasn't just we who had changed; our country had also changed in many ways.

Changes to a country take place gradually, and they may be almost imperceptible to people living there. But whenever we return to the United States from overseas after a four-year term, we have to face them all at once. The country we return to isn't the country that we left.

In this sense we identify with what the writer of Hebrews said. If Abraham and his descendants "had longed for the country they came from, they could have gone back. But they were looking for a better place, a heavenly homeland" (Heb. 11:15–16a).

We are far better off longing for the better country to come than thinking about the earthly country we left behind when we went to Brazil. When people ask me where our home is, more and more I think of my heavenly home. I know that it is only there that I will be completely at home.

— Cheryl Jensen

I took my troubles to the LORD

I CRIED OUT TO HIM

and he **answered** my prayer

— PSALM 120:1

Call upon the Lord

I took my troubles to the Lord; I cried out to him, and he answered my prayer.

— Psalm 120:1

"Lord God, I need you!" This was the cry of my heart on a night when all had fallen apart.

The last several months had been filled with emergency room visits for both my husband and youngest son. Not only had their health issues been scary, but also the bills were piling up. Then, while our eldest son was moving seven hundred miles away for a new job, his car broke down on the side of a major highway, leaving him stranded and in some danger. We immediately threw a change of clothes into a bag and drove almost three hundred miles to help him.

We learned we'd need to order parts and that it would be a $2,000 repair. We put the first $900 on our credit card (bringing it to its maximum) and paid the remaining $1,100 from our checkbook—before paying our bills.

In confidence I told God, "We are your missionaries. We are serving where you have called us. It will have to be you who provides from an unseen treasury."

We'd seen God provide miraculously several times in the eight years since we'd entered the mission field. Once, when we were short $400 to enter Wycliffe USA's training camp, God provided the funds three days before the deadline from someone who did not know our plight.

Another time, when we thought we were to serve in another country, we were $1,000 short the price of our airfare. A stranger entered our church, handed my husband an envelope containing ten $100 bills and left, never to be seen again.

Now, in faith, we called upon him again.

Within a day of driving the seven hundred miles home from our son's new location, we were given $1,500 in gifts, and more was promised. The bills were paid.

Just as his Word declares, God was and is faithful.

— Elise Armfield

> "We are your missionaries. We are serving where you have called us."

Don't be surprised
when I say

You
must
be
born
again

— JOHN 3:7

A New Heart

So don't be surprised when I say, "You must be born again."

— John 3:7

Pugong was a Filipino man who thought he knew what his life purpose was—until God changed his heart.

He was the foremost priest in the traditional religion of his Central Ifugao village. He believed in and understood the power of the spirits. The area where he lived was renowned for its allegiance to spirit worship, and when Bible translation began there in the 1960s, he witnessed intense spiritual warfare. But over time Pugong also came to understand the power of Christ.

He saw his nine children and many of his neighbors become believers, especially after the New Testament was published in Central Ifugao in 1980, and he experienced God's patient love for many years. His children never gave up on him; nor did the church; nor did I. In fact, I remember him telling me that when he saw my light on at night, he knew I probably wasn't willing to sleep until I knew he was safely home from performing his priestly duties, which included drinking large quantities of a traditional fermented brew.

"Yes, I'm going to accept Christ," Pugong said for many years. "But not yet. I'm still afraid of what the spirits will do to me." Finally Pugong found the courage to commit his fears to the Lord. When a church choir came to his home to sing for him, he announced, "I'm ready to accept Christ."

"Wait until a pastor comes!" they said.

"No, I don't need a pastor. I can pray now." And he did.

Four months later, with his new heart, Pugong squatted in a low drum of water and was baptized. His altar, rice god, and other traditional religious paraphernalia were all burned. At his invitation, his fellow priests were present. "I truly have become a follower of Christ," he told them, "and you must do the same."

It was a grand day! Scripture changes the way people think about God; it changes their worldview; it rewrites their road map so that it leads directly to the Father via the Son. And it results in changed lives for people like Pugong.

It's never easy to rewrite the road map we've decided to follow, but through the power of God it is possible. As long as we are alive, it's never too late for us or for someone who has followed pagan gods to turn to the one true God. But to do that, we have to be able to understand what he is saying to us. We have to understand his Word.

Pugong was born again.

— Anne West

GIVE TO THE LORD THE

GLORY

HE DESERVES!

God's House

*O nations of the world, recognize the L*ORD*, recognize that the L*ORD *is glorious and strong. Give to the L*ORD *the glory he deserves! Bring your offering and come into his presence. Worship the L*ORD *in all his holy splendor.*

— 1 Chronicles 16:28–29

For several weeks Maasai John had been our contact with members of the local Maasai community, as a number of them helped us and other families learn to live in a rural East African setting. Toward the end of our time together, Maasai John invited our family and one other to join his family for chai, or afternoon tea, in their compound.

The *manatta* (homestead) consisted of several dung-and-mud homes with stick roofs, forming a circle around an inner corral where a few cattle and restless goats were housed at night. These animals, gaunt and haggard, represented the full wealth and honor of John, his brothers, and their families.

Though John spoke English, the rest of his family did not. His family and our family did not speak a common language, but we shared a common love—a love for Jesus and, after just a few hours, a love for one another.

As we made our way back to the Jeep, John invited us to stop at one more building. This one was made of cinder blocks and cement with a tin roof. It had several benches and holes in the walls for windows. This was God's house. John had built it for his family to gather each week to worship God, study his Word, and learn to follow his Son.

Shortly after that holy afternoon, I learned that the common perception in the local rural area is that if you are poor you live in a mud hut, if you are more well-off you live in a wooden structure, and if you are wealthy you live in a stone house. John had built a stone palace for God, his king, while he and his loved ones continued to live in their humble mud homes.

— Carol Dowsett

> His family and our family did not speak a common language, but we shared a common love.

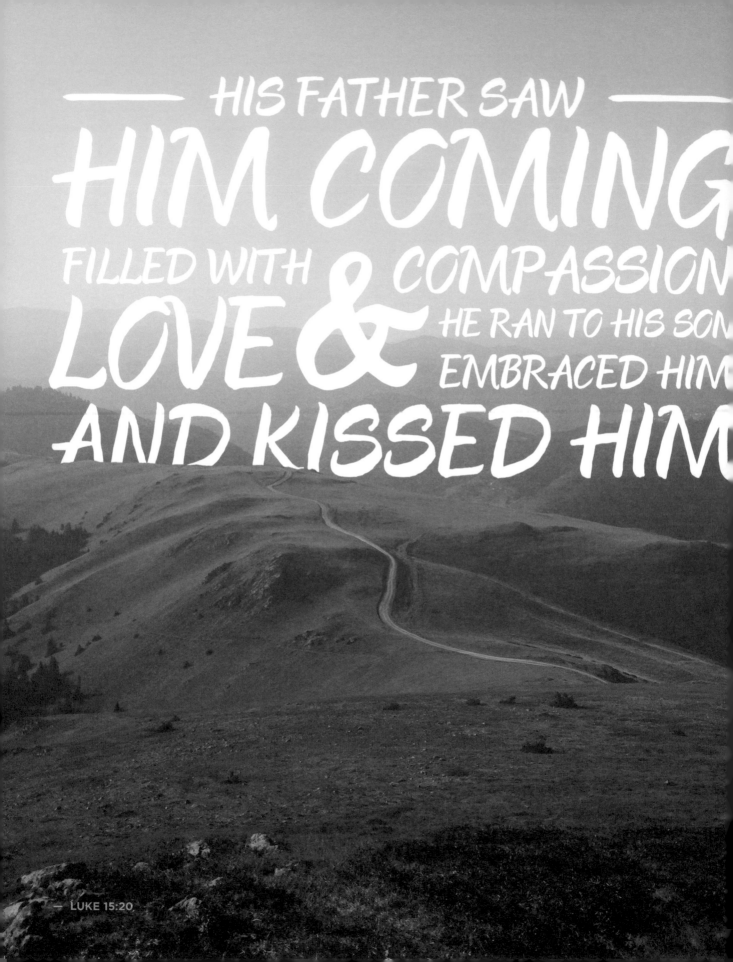

HIS FATHER SAW

HIM COMING

FILLED WITH & COMPASSION

LOVE HE RAN TO HIS SON

EMBRACED HIM

AND KISSED HIM

— LUKE 15:20

Filled with Love

So he returned home to his father. And while he was still a long way off, his father saw him coming. Filled with love and compassion, he ran to his son, embraced him, and kissed him.

— Luke 15:20

As I entered college at the end of my teenage years, I longed for freedom away from parents. Here was a great opportunity to satisfy my longing, by moving to a university three hundred miles away from home. Enjoying my own space, time, and relationships, I thought that freedom was synonymous with a quest for youthful pleasures and all that kind of life offered at the time.

I didn't grow up in a Christian home, so my moral compass was simply forged by the cultural definition of good and bad. I didn't realize that the poor company I kept would corrupt my character and jeopardize my academic pursuits. I was working on the downhill side of life when a classmate invited me to a student fellowship picnic. Out of respect for the classmate whose seemingly purpose-driven life had already challenged my lifestyle, I accepted the invitation.

At the picnic, the main activity that kept my attention was a study of the Parable of the Lost Son found in Luke 15:11–32. I was unfamiliar with God's Word, but the passage gave me a strong indication and conviction of my state as a "lost son." I could clearly identify with the prodigal son. Not only did I learn about my alienation from God, but I also got a clear understanding of God's loving heart and his readiness to welcome home the lost son that I was.

This intimate conviction was communicated to me particularly clearly in verse 20, "So he returned home to his father. And while he was still a long way off, his father saw him coming. Filled with love and compassion, he ran to his son, embraced him, and kissed him."

The father's exuberant love and embrace outweighed the guilt of the repentant and ashamed son. And there was a great feast and rejoicing.

In this world, we live with the cruel realities of rejection, hatred, shame, and guilt. Some of these may result from our own wrongdoings or from other experiences in our family, workplace, neighborhood, or in society in general. These realities create deep longings that we sometimes seek to satisfy in futile ways, like broken cisterns that can't hold water.

But we can remember that, in God, there is a spring of living water, a source of endless love and compassion. With an uncritical heart, he is ever ready with arms wide open to embrace us and meet our deepest longings. Wisdom is turning to him and finding our satisfaction in him alone.

— Michel Kenmogne

OUR CHILDREN

WILL ALSO SERVE HIM

Future generations

WILL HEAR ABOUT

THE

Wonders

OF THE LORD

HIS RIGHTEOUS ACTS

WILL BE TOLD TO THOSE NOT YET BORN

THEY WILL HEAR ABOUT EVERYTHING

HE HAS DONE

— PSALM 22:30-31

For Those Coming Behind Us

Our children will also serve him. Future generations will hear about the wonders of the LORD. His righteous acts will be told to those not yet born. They will hear about everything he has done.

— *Psalm 22:30–31*

"When you translate so simply, you don't respect God's Word! Even little children can understand it!"

The Cheke Holo New Testament review committee fell silent at this outburst. This was the final review of the Scripture translation before it would be published for the Cheke Holo people, and indeed a very critical point of decision making. The committee was working to ensure that the translation represented accuracy to the source text, clarity in word choices and reading, and naturalness in terms of how the people spoke in everyday language.

Now one member of the group was openly criticizing Andrew, the lead translator, for his consistent methodology of making the Word accessible and understandable in their language. How would they deal with this sudden challenge that was so dramatically and openly presented before them?

Andrew calmly replied, "Thank you for telling me that the translation is clear, so clear in fact, that children can understand it. You see, when I was translating, all the way through that task I was thinking about my seven children. I was making word choices and grammar choices that they would understand. You and I need to face the fact that we are getting old, and won't be around much longer. This translation is not really for us; it's for those coming behind us."

We often think of Bible translation as a tool God can use for immediate impact. There is no doubt that stories reflecting this purpose abound, and we praise God repeatedly for this. But it is also helpful to remember that a meaningful Scripture translation is something that the Lord can use for many years to come, even something that is prepared and waiting for those yet unborn.

Can we trust him, with eyes and hearts of faith, that the good seed of his Word will bear fruit not only in this generation, but also in generations to come?

— Freddy Boswell

A meaningful Scripture translation is something that the Lord can use for many years to come.

Their words are like a lamp

SHINING IN A DARK PLACE

— 2 PETER 1:19

God's Light in a Dark Place

*Because of that experience, we have even greater confidence in the message
proclaimed by the prophets. You must pay close attention to what they wrote, for
their words are like a lamp shining in a dark place—until the Day dawns, and Christ the
Morning Star shines in your hearts.*

— 2 Peter 1:19

I have seen darkness. It was in a refugee camp in Darfur, where I was working for World Vision. For many people, Darfur is synonymous with conflict, pain, and despair. It is the essence of what the Bible refers to as darkness, but I also witnessed God's glory and an abundance of his light. It was there that I met a boy, then six years old. His name was Adam, and he and his mother, Nazarene, were living in the camp.

He had been born in a village of mud huts, the same village where his mother and father had been born. When I met Adam, he was silent—unable to speak. Nine months earlier he'd witnessed his father being brutally murdered by members of a militia. They then sexually assaulted his mother and burned the village. Adam hadn't spoken since.

In that scrappy refugee camp, Nazarene delivered the infant the rapists had bequeathed to her. Looking back, I reflect on the words of Job, "If my misery could be weighed and my troubles be put on the scales, they would outweigh all the sands of the sea" (Job 6:2–3).

The consequences of that evil, however, were overpowered by the glory of God I saw in Nazarene. When I asked her how I might pray for her, she smiled and said, "Pray that I can forgive those who killed my husband. Pray that God will forgive them. Pray for the men who gave me this child. Pray that they will seek God's forgiveness, and that I will see them in heaven."

God is with Nazarene and Adam. His Spirit spoke through them to me—words of a love so deep that even the most barbarous acts of mankind were drowned in it.

I had gone to Sudan to serve God, but he was serving me. Like the prophetic words in 2 Peter, "the Day dawns, and Christ the Morning Star shines," Nazarene left an indelible image in my mind. God's Word heals the wounds of trauma.

God shines his immeasurable light and love in some of the darkest places on earth. He creates light. His Word brings light and pierces the darkness. While evil is a powerful force, God's love shall always prevail.

— Atul Tandon

God shines his immeasurable light and love in some of the darkest places on earth.

My *future* is in

your
hands

In His Hands

My future is in your hands.

— Psalm 31:15a

My wife, Dallas, and I recently had a brief visit from an old friend from high school. John was writing a book and wanted to talk with us about our walk toward a career with Wycliffe Bible Translators focused on overcoming Bible poverty—the lack of access to clear, accurate, and natural Bible translation.

Revisiting that period of our lives with him—looking back over more than thirty years of ministry—was surprisingly refreshing.

"What was attractive about Wycliffe?" he asked.

Their dedication to providing for others what we have—the Bible!

"How hard was it to leave family and friends to move overseas?"

It was hard, but it became harder to stay in the familiar than to move into an uncertain future where we knew God was calling us.

"How did you choose Cameroon?"

We didn't; God directed us there! Really, we didn't even know where Cameroon was when we were first told there was a need there.

The walk through these memories of decisions made in those early years made us realize that they still shape our lives today. We had a deep-seated belief, like the Psalmist says, that our times were in his hands, not our own.

Our conversation with John circled a lot around the messiness of life, including how our walk as Jesus's followers led to a career that most would not have predicted for us, and how applying his teaching in our lives made it an exciting adventure.

"How did you see God in your everyday circumstances, and did this influence you?"

We are, and have always been, rooted in our experience of God's faithfulness and in our love for his eternal Word, which has been the light and lamp for our lives. We believe others have the right to have it too. (In fact, we believe it's unjust for them not to have it.)

Retelling our journey to John made me realize that there were sound theological and biblical principles behind the choices we made, and God's hand had guided every step.

Lord, thank you for your Word that is alive and powerful, sharper than the sharpest two-edged sword, cutting between my soul and spirit, between my joints and marrow. It exposes my innermost thoughts and desires (Heb. 4:12).

It will last forever.

My hope is that when you look back on your journey, you'll see circumstances that were clearly God-ordained and glorifying to him. Let's start today by looking to his Word to direct our steps, acknowledging that our future truly is in his hands.

— Bob Creson

A PERSON WHO IS PUT —IN— CHARGE AS A MANAGER MUST —BE— FAITH FUL

— 1 CORINTHIANS 4:2 —

A Faithful Servant

Now, a person who is put in charge as a manager must be faithful. As for me, it matters very little how I might be evaluated by you or by any human authority. . . . It is the Lord himself who will examine me and decide.

— 1 Corinthians 4:2–4

I was born and raised in southern Mexico in a remote, hot, and humid village. My parents, Phil and Mary Baer, were translators there among the Lacandone people. I have fond memories of the Lacandones, a people who were content to live by hunting wild game and cutting down a small area of the forest to grow corn.

I do not, however, have fond memories of memorizing Bible verses during those years. I was terrible at it. My brother, on the other hand, had a terrific memory. In fact, one day as a punishment for fighting, we were given a choice to memorize Romans 8 or take a spanking. I started to memorize but soon gave up. I took the spanking—gladly.

There is one verse, however, that I never attempted to memorize, but I remember it well, fifty years later—1 Corinthians 4:2. The Lacandone people were steeped in their practice of worshipping small clay-pot idols. Year after year, the Lacandones rejected the Bible message. In fact one Lacandone was brutally honest. "You'll never get a Lacandone to believe," he snarled one day at my dad.

I remember visiting American churches with my parents on furlough. A good friend asked my dad, "Are there any believers among the Lacandones yet?" With sadness in his eyes my dad whispered, "No." The next question was just as difficult. "Are you going back?" My dad lifted his head, and his eyes brightened as he responded, "Yes!" He continued, "First Corinthians 4:2 says, 'What is required of a manager is that he be found faithful.' The results are in the Lord's hands. God requires us to be faithful and promises to honor his Word."

That faithfulness would be tested. It was twenty years before the Lacandones put their faith and trust in Jesus Christ. In 1979 the New Testament translation was finally completed, and several churches continue to flourish today!

Is there an area of your life in which you have not seen fruit but are being called to be faithful? Follow your calling and trust God for the outcome. It will be worth it all.

— Phil Baer Jr.

"God requires us to be faithful and promises to honor his Word."

LET ALL
THAT I AM
PRAISE
THE LORD
WITH MY WHOLE HEART
I WILL PRAISE HIS
holy name

Manna in the Tropical Wilderness

*Let all that I am praise the L*ORD*; with my whole heart, I will praise his holy name. . . . He fills my life with good things.*

— Psalm 103:1, 5a

A week before Christmas, I wrote in my journal, "This may well be the worst Christmas ever." I was low-spirited from, among other things, the monotony of island food. I like taro and yams just fine, but eating them every day gets old. There are no markets on the small island where my family works in Bible translation and linguistics. The main gardens are a two-to-three-hour walk away, so people usually carry back starchy staples rather than fruits and vegetables. On this day I was fantasizing about a fresh green salad with cherry tomatoes. I wrote in my journal that I would give anything for a big, crunchy cucumber.

After writing my journal entry, I set out on a walk with our toddler, Alexander. A neighbor woman approached us with a bundle wrapped in banana leaves. Inside were green onions, several stalks of a local vegetable they call "island cabbage," and one large, firm cucumber.

"The Master [God] told me to set this aside for you," she said. She laughed when I told her how I'd been craving cucumber.

That evening we received another gift from a neighbor—a beautiful ripe watermelon. But God wasn't through wowing me yet. We got one more rare gift the following day—a bundle of watercress, the only local salad green. With a vinaigrette dressing, it tastes delightful.

On Christmas day we had just a few treats to put in our stockings and a couple presents that actually arrived in time from loved ones. Though our Christmas lacked the usual pile of presents, we received a more lasting gift: the knowledge that God is not too busy to meet even our most trivial needs.

Indeed, I think he took great delight in sending along that cucumber, and in following it up with more treats just for good measure. He is reminding me that although my joy does not reside in my physical circumstances, still he delights to care for me even in these small things.

— Danielle Smith

My joy does not reside in my physical circumstances.

LIVE CLEAN
INNOCENT LIVES
AS CHILDREN
OF GOD

shining like bright lights

Complimentary Insult

Live clean, innocent lives as children of God, shining like bright lights in a world full of crooked and perverse people. Hold firmly to the word of life.

— Philippians 2:15b–16a

"*Jarti, bela kabda. Sagale na keni!*" Though I was a stranger in this culture, I had learned enough of the local language, Gabbra, to clearly understand what this man was saying. "Old woman, I am hungry. Give me food!"

Right off I bristled. "Thirty-five is not that old," I assured myself. "First he insults my appearance and then demands food as though I were his servant!" I held my tongue but boiled inside.

God immediately brought a Scripture to mind: "Do everything without complaining and arguing, so that no one can criticize you. Live clean, innocent lives as children of God, shining like bright lights in a world full of crooked and perverse people. Hold firmly to the word of life" (Phil. 2:14–16a).

Rebuked, I answered God, "Yes, Lord, no grumbling and no disputing. I am your servant, holding out the Word of life."

Adjusting to a nomadic African culture seemed as disorienting to me as adjusting to life on Mars! Nearly everything seemed backward, upside down, and flipped from right to left. One day even the bathwater seemed to swirl the wrong direction as it flowed down the drain. These seemingly inconsequential events had mounted up to major stressors. Culture shock had struck, leaving my normally calm and collected self feeling irritable and on edge; but God's Word spoke clearly.

Two years later I finally came to understand that the man had addressed me with honor, in effect calling me a wise woman, as opposed to a silly girl. As for the demand for food, the Gabbra language has no word for "please," so one simply states his or her needs honestly. Actually, I was the one who had made the faux pas. Any considerate woman in this culture would have immediately offered water and food to a visitor who walked in from the hot desert sands.

When people enter new cultures or stressful times of any sort, innocent words and actions can seem wrong, even insulting. Thankfully, the Lord remains faithful to bring relevant Scripture to mind at crucial junctures. I shudder to think what kind of mess this old woman could have caused during the early years of our language project, when even a compliment sounded like an insult.

— Dorothea Lander

"Yes, Lord, no grumbling and no disputing. I am your servant, holding out the Word of life."

Anyone
who welcomes
a little child
like this
on my behalf
welcomes

me

— MARK 9:37

A New Season

Anyone who welcomes a little child like this on my behalf welcomes me, and anyone who welcomes me welcomes not only me but also my Father who sent me.

— Mark 9:37

My husband, Derwin, and I have known for years that God is faithful and good. The difference now is that we have grown to depend on that fact as our lifeline like we've never done before.

We recently decided to adopt three siblings from foster care. That changed their lives and ours. After twenty-four years of marriage, Derwin and I had grown used to our predictable schedule and structured way of life with no children. Then after reading an article about kids who age out of foster care without ever being adopted, we thought, "Well, we can do something to help one child. That's something we can do." We did not count on the reality that children are often part of sibling groups. So we told God we would help one child, but he clearly said "three," and he always wins.

That was the end of our predictable existence. Now the passage we are clinging to and standing on is Mark 9:37, "Anyone who welcomes a little child like this on my behalf welcomes me, and anyone who welcomes me welcomes not only me but also my Father who sent me."

They are brilliant children, probably something they inherited. And they have a heightened sense of awareness, always alert to what is going on around them. This is probably a result of the many trials they experienced, and their constant struggle to figure out what twists or turns life would present next. They are cunning, wise, full of fury, and hungry for love and affirmation, yet unwilling to accept it at times. They are a complex puzzle that only God fully understands. With three of them acting and reacting to one another and to us, our lives are in full-on adventure mode all the time.

When we welcomed our three children, we welcomed the Son and the Father into our household in new and powerful ways. God has given us wisdom, encouragement, and new meaning for our lives. He has answered prayers so clearly and immediately. He has given us peace in turmoil, strength in trials, and his divine love in our hearts.

This new family is a new season for all of us; and we love each other, with God's help, unconditionally.

We are so grateful for the Word of God in this experience. It informed us, prepared us, gave us something to stand on. We saw God's promises come to life. It's almost impossible for us to imagine going through all of this without the knowledge of God and his Word. And yet millions of people go through challenging experiences every day without this awesome book.

It's clear to us now that we must work tirelessly to get the Word to everyone, so children and families can have new life, so those in trials can have peace, and so everyone who would respond to the call can be grafted into the grace-filled family tree of God.

— Wendy Scott-Penson

Your
WORD
is a lamp
to
guide
MY FEET
and a light
for
my
path

— PSALM 119:105

Transitions

Your word is a lamp to guide my feet and a light for my path.

— Psalm 119:105

"Was that you whispering, Lord?"

It had been a disquieting month. I felt God might be calling me to transition from one ministry to another, but I was not certain and didn't want to proceed without consulting the Word. Robbi, my bride, and I had agreed that we would read the book of Isaiah for thirty days so as to discern a confirmation from God. Isaiah is my favorite book in the Bible. I had come to appreciate this book as it had been involved in many of my previous life transitions.

All month long I had not heard anything. As I moved toward Isaiah chapter 62, I wondered, "Will the Lord speak through the Scripture? How will he speak? And how will I know?"

It was the beginning of the new millennium; I was in China with my family as we customarily spent every other summer there so that we could learn about the culture and the ministry that I was involved in. In my quiet time in the morning, I read Isaiah 62 through verse 10, on to verses 11 and 12. Then I felt the Lord quietly whispering to me.

I retraced the words back up the page and reread verse 10, "Go out through the gates! Prepare the highway for my people to return! Smooth out the road; pull out the boulders;

raise a flag for all the nations to see."

Was this the verse confirming the transition? I meditated upon it, and the sense of that internal whisper from God was firm, loud, and clear! I knew I was supposed to act upon it. "Wow!" I thought. "Is that how the Word speaks today?"

In obedience to the Word of God, Robbi and I completed the transition into our new ministry over the next fifteen months. This might seem like a long time, but God knew the time necessary for a proper and good transition. With each of our questions or concerns, he directed our steps: Should we remain in Asia? How do we handle changes to our financial provision? How do we faithfully and gracefully let go of this old and comfortable position, and receive the new role?

What I did not know at the time was that God would also provide Isaiah 62:10 for the upcoming years in this new ministry. Every phrase within this poetic verse came into being, and I understood the significance of it over the years as I moved through the assignment with the new ministry.

Are you in a transition today? Are you seeking guidance in Scripture? The Word of God is alive. Are you ready to receive his Word?

— Samuel Chiang

BY HIS DIVINE POWER GOD HAS GIVEN US EVERYTHING WE NEED FOR LIVING A GODLY LIFE. WE HAVE RECEIVED ALL OF THIS BY COMING TO KNOW HIM.

— 2 PETER 1:3

Using Your Influence

By his divine power, God has given us everything we need for living a godly life. We have received all of this by coming to know him, the one who called us to himself by means of his marvelous glory and excellence.

— 2 Peter 1:3

Over the course of my life, I have come to realize that God oftentimes chooses to grace people with far more than they could have ever imagined.

Years ago I asked God for his blessing, favor, and wisdom. When I began a career in the NFL, I quickly saw God answering that prayer. My successes on the field and my influence in the community were increasing year by year. Of course some of that was the expected outcome of simply being a professional athlete, in the prime of his career and at the top of his game. But God's grace and favor were so apparent to me in my physical health and performance.

I also believe God sovereignly chose to give me success on the field, because it would give me greater credibility off the field in my community. My success afforded me the opportunity to be with influential people—the kind of people most would consider the "kings" of my community.

Meanwhile, God introduced my wife and me to the work of Bible translation. Our eyes were opened to the plight of the Bibleless—the poorest of the poor, the "very least of these." He broke our hearts for the nations.

Over and over I read Isaiah 61:1–2, "The Spirit of the Sovereign Lord is upon me, for the Lord has anointed me to bring good news to the poor. He has sent me to comfort the brokenhearted and to proclaim that captives will be released and prisoners will be freed. He has sent me to tell those who mourn that the time of the Lord's favor has come, and with it, the day of God's anger against their enemies."

I came to the conclusion that the influence I had would either help me build my own kingdom or build God's kingdom. I decided the focus of my life was to be sharing the good news of the gospel, being a voice for the voiceless and a defender of the defenseless.

Scripture has transformed my life! I went from wanting "power" in this world for my own benefit, to wanting to help others encounter the true power of the gospel by seeing Jesus face-to-face. God tells us in 2 Peter 1:3 that he gives us, through his divine power, everything we need in life to do what he calls us to do. I have decided to use the influence he gives me to encourage, bless, and empower others, and not to focus on myself.

Whether you've been entrusted with a lot or a little influence, how are you using that opportunity? Whose kingdom are you serving?

— Todd Peterson

fan
into
flames
the
spiritual gift
G**O**D
GAVE YOU

— 2 TIMOTHY 1:6

Fan into Flames

This is why I remind you to fan into flames the spiritual gift God gave you when I laid my hands on you. For God has not given us a spirit of fear and timidity, but of power, love, and self-discipline.

— 2 Timothy 1:6–7

"What have you done to my husband?" The words spilled out of the young woman's mouth as she burst through the door into Yepo and Marcelina's home. "Victor came back from the recording session a completely different person. You must have spoken to him harshly or knocked him around a bit in order for such a drastic change to take place!"

Yepo, one of the translators for Scripture in the Huaylas Quechua language, had met Victor several years earlier at a literacy workshop and remembered him as a dedicated young Christian who was an exceptionally good reader. At Yepo's recent invitation, Victor had left his village and traveled to the capital city to take part in recording a dramatic reading of the newly translated Huaylas Quechua New Testament. He was a good reader, but Victor had stumbled in his Christian walk and was not living as a godly husband and father.

One morning during the recording sessions, the men read through Paul's reminder of Timothy's godly upbringing, and Paul's admonition to "fan into flames the spiritual gift" of God that Timothy possessed (2 Tim. 1:6). Tears streamed down Victor's face as he recognized how far he had strayed from his own godly upbringing. He recommitted his life to Christ that day.

No one had preached to Victor; no one had knocked him around or spoken harshly to him. The changes that Victor's wife noticed as soon as he returned home were results of the gentle voice of God himself, speaking to Victor in the language of his heart.

What about you? Have some of the flames in your heart died down to mere embers? Perhaps the joy of your salvation isn't quite as front and center as it used to be. Or maybe bitterness or a lack of forgiveness has crept in to replace the love that once resided there. Maybe just the busyness of daily life has drawn you away from a close relationship with your Lord.

Take heart; the embers are still glowing. And take a moment right now to fan those embers back into flame by spending some time listening to God's voice in the language of your heart.

— Rachel Yanac

Have some of the flames in your heart died down to mere embers?

AFTER THIS I SAW A VAST CROWD

TOO GREAT TO COUNT

FROM

EVERY NATION

AND

TRIBE

AND

PEOPLE

AND

LANGUAGE

STANDING IN FRONT OF THE THRONE

AND BEFORE THE LAMB

— REVELATION 7:9

Every Nation, Tribe, People, and Language

After this I saw a vast crowd, too great to count, from every nation and tribe and people and language, standing in front of the throne and before the Lamb. . . . And they were shouting with a great roar, "Salvation comes from our God who sits on the throne and from the Lamb!"
— Revelation 7:9a–10

As a young university student, I lived with the sole purpose of pursuing the American dream—a multibillion-dollar professional vocation that would land me the perfect job, which would land me the perfect home and material possessions, which would land me the happiness that I was desperately searching for.

I invested all my time and resources into this dream. I shaped my identity around it. I chased the dream until one day, when it was finally within reach, I encountered the Word of God on my college campus, and it *blew me away*. Through a weekly Bible study on campus and a renewed commitment to reading the Scriptures daily, I began to see a different purpose for living. Through God's Word, I began to see his love for the world and his mission to bless all people groups on earth.

I began to see that from Genesis to Revelation, our God is a missionary God. Revelation 7:9–10 describes this glorious image of diverse language groups and tribes, all coming before the throne of God in worship, too many people to count!

After engaging in the Scriptures, I heard God call me to pioneer evangelical student ministry in Mongolia—a country that in 1989 had only one known Christian convert in the entire country.

I arrived in Mongolia in 2002, and what I saw was inspiring. The New Testament had just been translated into Mongolian and published in the 1990s, and the Old Testament translation was completed in 2000. Then the church exploded. Within a few years of the complete Bible being available, there were more than one hundred twenty churches and twenty-five thousand believers, due in large part to the fact that Mongolians could now read and hear Scripture in a language they clearly understood.

In my own student ministry, I owe much gratitude to those who worked so hard to translate the Scriptures into Mongolian, because without them I would not have been able to share the gospel with Mongolians. Hundreds of students came before the Lord every morning, drinking up the Scriptures like water. Students who owned their own Bible would treasure it and read it daily, while others showed up at our office each day to read a copy.

And it wasn't just in student ministry. We saw Bible translation being a pipeline for many other ministries. Believers rely on the translations for their church-planting ministries, discipleship programs, and medical outreaches. Bible translation isn't an optional ministry, but has been a necessary ministry for the furthering of the church in Mongolia.

One day, we will see Mongolians as a part of the Revelation 7 picture of every nation, tribe, people, and language coming before the throne. May it be so!

— Tom Lin

WHOEVER IS THE LEAST AMONG YOU IS

THE greatest

— LUKE 9:48

Being Last

Then his disciples began arguing about which of them was the greatest. But Jesus knew their thoughts, so he brought a little child to his side. Then he said to them, "Anyone who welcomes a little child like this on my behalf welcomes me, and anyone who welcomes me also welcomes my Father who sent me. Whoever is the least among you is the greatest."

— Luke 9:46–48

In my Bible translation work, I normally enjoy checking passages for understanding with the local community. However, recently this joy was tested. I set out to find Joanne, my favorite person to check verses with, hoping she'd be home and available for twenty or thirty minutes. When I arrived, she greeted me nicely, and I sat down.

Joanne runs a store out of her home. Before we could start checking any Bible passages, a man arrived, wanting to make a purchase. After what seemed like an eternity (maybe fifteen or twenty minutes in reality) I was looking for signs that this customer might be leaving.

But just as she was wrapping things up with him, another woman arrived. Their conversation went on and on! My longer-than-usual list of to-dos started running through my head. I began to heat up and fret about this situation.

Mentally running through my options, I thought that if I went home, Joanne would likely think I was angry. If I moved into the store to make my presence bigger, it would be rude. I felt trapped in her house with no way to redeem the time. I tried to pray, but my agitated spirit interfered.

I started guessing what Joanne might be trying to communicate to me indirectly by ignoring me, but concluded that both women were just being completely present in their conversation—relationship being the priority.

In my culture, the person who is first in line has priority. I was considering myself first and of higher priority than the lady who had arrived after me. I wanted Joanne to attend to me.

Mental and spiritual relief came, as it often does, from God's Word. Just days before, I'd checked Luke 9:46–48, in which the disciples have a tiff with each other about who is more important. It ends with Jesus's declaration, "Whoever is the least among you is the greatest."

While my hostess and her customer were likely not aware, I was having a major tiff with them about which of us was most important.

Jesus calmed me and kept me seated by whispering that if I would submit to being "last," the Father would consider me great. I wanted to be great in God's eyes, so I sat and sat. After about an hour and a half, Joanne gave me her attention, good suggestions for improving the passage, and a much-needed lesson in being last.

— Julie Andersen

SO,
BE TRULY GLAD
THERE IS
WONDERFUL
JOY
AHEAD
EVEN THOUGH
YOU MUST ENDURE
MANY
TRIALS
FOR
A
LITTLE
WHILE

— 1 PETER 1:6

Shaped and Strengthened

So be truly glad. There is wonderful joy ahead, even though you must endure many trials for a little while. These trials will show that your faith is genuine. It is being tested as fire tests and purifies gold—though your faith is far more precious than mere gold. So when your faith remains strong through many trials, it will bring you much praise and glory and honor on the day when Jesus Christ is revealed to the whole world.

— *1 Peter 1:6-7*

It may be that you wonder why you go through trials and sickness and weakness and tribulations. Let me mention an experience I had in Guatemala when I was just beginning the study of the Cakchiquel language.

I was sitting in the primitive shelter that served us as the bedroom, dining room, kitchen, and workroom. I looked out the door (there were no windows) and saw Tata Miguel, the headman of the clan and owner of the little hut that we were in, holding a stick in the fire. I thought, "What is Tata Miguel up to? If he wants to burn that stick, why doesn't he throw it in?" But no, he held it and turned it around, and then he took it over to the fork of a tree and pulled it this way and that way.

And so I went over to investigate. I found that Tata Miguel had cut a young sapling that was of a good type of wood for a hoe handle but wasn't shaped the way he wanted it. He used the heat of the fire to soften up the wood, and then bent it in the strong fork of a tree, making a hoe handle that was shaped correctly and would last longer.

Dear one, I believe the only way (apart from the work of the Holy Spirit and the Bible) for us to become strong and shaped in the way that Christ can best use us, is through tests of one kind or another. So, let's let our God hold us in the flame and pull us this way and that against the hard stresses of life.

— William Cameron Townsend

> I believe the only way (apart from the work of the Holy Spirit and the Bible) for us to become strong and shaped in the way that Christ can best use us, is through tests.

129

NOTES

MEET BOB CRESON

*B*ob is the president and CEO of Wycliffe Bible Translators USA and firmly believes there is nothing God can't express in the language people use every day. He and his wife, Dallas, have served in Bible translation for more than thirty years, including several years in Cameroon and Chad, West Africa. He also wrote *The Finish Line: Stories of Hope Through Bible Translation*.

In addition to his work with Wycliffe USA, Bob has contributed to Bible translation in a variety of roles in SIL International (one of Wycliffe's primary partners), the Seed Company (a Wycliffe affiliate organization), and Every Tribe Every Nation (a partnership of ministries committed to ending Bible poverty), among others.

He and Dallas have four adult children and one grandchild. They live in Orlando, Florida, where Bob enjoys eating breakfast on the lanai, reading books on missiology, singing Beach Boys songs with his grandson, and sharing both fun and vision on social media.

MEET THE CONTRIBUTORS

JULIE ANDERSEN

Julie and her husband, Gerry, came to treasure the Word of God after life's challenges revealed their need to always center their minds on God's truth. This passion led them to Bible translation, where they enjoy the privilege of serving through Wycliffe and the Mexico branch of SIL—first among the Totonac people and more recently in personnel and publications.

ELISE ARMFIELD

Elise served the Lord faithfully for more than ten years as a missionary with Wycliffe USA. She supported her fellow missionaries in countless ways, including as one of Wycliffe's dedicated prayer warriors. After a battle with breast cancer, Elise passed away in January 2014. She is survived by her husband, Joe, who still serves with Wycliffe today, and their two adult sons, one of whom is also serving Wycliffe along with his wife.

PHIL BAER JR.

Phil and his wife, Sarah, have worked for forty-two years with Wycliffe, SIL, and JAARS, in Cameroon, the United States, and Mexico.

Today Phil works in Scripture engagement in Mexico. His parents completed the New Testament and a summary of the Old Testament in a language group in Mexico. Having been raised in a remote village, Phil has seen the power of the Word translated and shared with an unreached people group. He has committed his life to translation and reaching the indigenous oral societies of the world.

JENI BISTER

Jeni and her husband, Mikael, have been working with the Nyungwe translation team in Mozambique since 1999. They have three children who know Africa as home. Jeni's most recent activities are in promoting mother-tongue educational activities and materials through small community reading groups. Jeni and Mikael believe that reading more means reading better, leading to opening God's Word and knowing his heart for all people.

FREDDY BOSWELL

Freddy is the former executive director of SIL International, an organization that serves people groups worldwide in sustainable language development. Freddy's service in linguistics and Bible translation has included nine years in the Solomon Islands, several of which he spent as a linguist and translation advisor to the Cheke Holo language group.

ADAM BOYD

Adam and his wife, Martha, met in Quito, Ecuador, where Adam experienced a radical conversion to Christianity and was called by God to the work of Bible translation. They have been serving as Bible translators among the Enga people of Papua New Guinea since 2012 and are committed to helping people receive Scripture in a language they can clearly understand.

JUDY BRANKS

Judy and her husband, Tom, recently retired after fifty-five years of service with Wycliffe. Their primary assignment was as linguists and translators for the Guambiano, an indigenous group of farmers in the Andes Mountains in Colombia. Judy said their time living with their five children among the Guambiano were the best years of their lives. They helped translate the New Testament, an Old Testament summary, and recordings of three hundred hymns and songs. Tom worked in administration when they were no longer able to live with the Guambiano.

SAMUEL CHIANG

Samuel is the president and CEO of the Seed Company, an organization launched by Wycliffe USA to accelerate Bible translation.

He has a wide range of experience with the global church, having traveled to over eighty countries and ministering in almost forty of them. He has written on China, Asia, persecution, innovation, and orality, and has published extensively.

GEORGE COWAN

George has a long history in Bible translation as a missionary to the Mazatec speakers in Mexico, former director of SIL International's Mexico branch, former president of Wycliffe Bible Translators International (now the Wycliffe Global Alliance), and director of linguistics schools in Canada, England, Germany, and the United States. Perhaps one of his best-known contributions to Bible translation has been his faithful work as a prayer warrior. George recently celebrated his one hundreth birthday.

STEVE DOUGLASS

Steve is president of both Campus Crusade for Christ International and Cru, as the ministry is known in the United States. He serves on the boards of several organizations. He is the author or coauthor of several books, including *Managing Yourself, How to Achieve Your Potential and Enjoy Life, How to Get Better Grades and Have More Fun,* and *Enjoying Your Walk with God.* His radio program, *Making Your Life Count,* airs daily on over eight hundred stations.

CAROL DOWSETT

Carol met Christ in high school while reading a contemporary English translation of the New Testament. From that moment on she knew the value of Scriptures available in everyday language. When God called her and her husband, Jim, into missions, Wycliffe and Bible translation were the natural fit. Carol led communications efforts in Africa and then at international levels for over fifteen years. She now serves as a communication consultant while Jim assists with sign language Bible translation.

BILLY GRAHAM

As a world-renowned evangelist and author, Billy Graham has preached the gospel to more people in live audiences than anyone else in history—nearly 215 million people in more than 185 countries and territories, and hundreds of millions more through television, video, film, and webcasts. He's a longtime friend to William Cameron Townsend and an advocate of the ministry of Bible translation.

DIANA GREEN

Diana and her husband, Harold, served with Wycliffe in Brazil for forty-nine years. They put the Palikur language into written form, taught the people to read and write, and translated the New Testament into their language. As translation consultants they also had a significant part in checking and approving translations in thirty-five other languages, which now have New Testaments or full Bibles in print.

MART GREEN

Mart is the founder of Mardel, a chain of Christian and education supply stores and of Every Tribe Entertainment, which produced movies *End of the Spear* and *Beyond the Gates of Splendor*. His family also started Hobby Lobby, and he now serves as the board chair. Currently Mart is helping build a digital Bible library through an alliance called Every Tribe Every Nation, in which Wycliffe is a partner.

RANDY GROFF

Randy joined Wycliffe Bible Translators in 1977 and helped translate the New Testament into the Jula language of Côte d'Ivoire. Today he works with Wycliffe and SIL International as a translation consultant in Nigeria. He also supports translation teams by producing exegetical aides and translation guides called Translator's Notes.

JON HAMPSHIRE

Jon and his wife, Cindi, joined Wycliffe Bible Translators in 1988, and God led them to serve in the Democratic Republic of the Congo in the heart of Africa. Jon has a passion to see Congolese people's lives transformed through a clear understanding of God's Word in their heart languages. Jon serves as the communications coordinator for SIL Eastern Congo Group.

RUSS HERSMAN

Russ and his wife, Lynda, joined Wycliffe in 1976 hoping to provide Scriptures to just one people group somewhere in the world. That desire took them to southern Sudan, where they spent twenty years supporting translation work for not one, but many people groups! Today Russ serves as the chief operations officer at Wycliffe USA.

JERRY JACKSON

After serving as missionaries on the Hopi and Navajo reservations, Jerry and his wife, Anet, founded Hosanna, now known as Faith Comes By Hearing. The ministry became a pioneer in audio Scripture production and engagement. Today the ministry offers audio Bibles through state-of-the-art technology and has provided audio Bible access, free of charge, to millions of people worldwide. Jerry is the author of *Get God's Word to Every Person* and *The Ark*.

CHERYL JENSEN

Cheryl and her husband, Al, have spent the past forty years serving God through the work of Bible translation. Besides serving as part of the translation team for the Wayampi people of Brazil, Cheryl has aided the translation for other people groups through linguistics consulting and through the training of both mother-tongue and non-indigenous Bible translators.

MICHEL KENMOGNE

Michel is passionate about Bible translation and literacy work, and has devoted his life to serving God and people. He is the first African to be elected as the executive director of SIL International and is the former associate director for Wycliffe Global Alliance Africa Area. Born in Cameroon, West Africa, Michel has long worked in translation and language development there.

DOROTHEA LANDER

God used growing up on a farm to prepare Dorothea for living with nomadic herders in sub-Saharan Africa. She and her husband, Jim, with their three children helped make the Bible available in a form that the Borana people could understand. Now in their thirty-second year with Wycliffe, Jim coordinates a Greek project that helps translators worldwide, and Dorothea writes to involve more people in Bible translation.

TOM LIN

Tom is passionate about God's Word and mobilizing people to serve God's global mission. He currently serves as the president of InterVarsity Christian Fellowship. Previously Tom served for nine years as a board member and vice of chair of Wycliffe USA. He is also the former vice president of missions for InterVarsity, and the former director of Urbana, one of the largest student missions conferences in the world. Tom is the author of *Pursuing God's Call* and *Losing Face, Finding Grace*.

ARETTA LOVING

Aretta went to Papua New Guinea with her husband, Ed, in 1959, where they translated the New Testament into the Awa language. They lived with the Awas until they finished the translation in 1974. Later they worked in Kenya, where Aretta was a writer and editor. Aretta has written three books and numerous articles. She now lives near JAARS in Waxhaw, North Carolina.

BERNIE MAY

Bernie is a former president of Wycliffe USA, former president of JAARS, an organization that helps provide practical, day-to-day support for Bible translation, and founder of the Seed Company, an organization launched by Wycliffe USA to accelerate Bible translation worldwide. He began his missionary career as a pilot flying other missionaries to remote locations in South America. Bernie wrote *Under His Wing* and *Learning to Trust* about his experiences as a pilot.

JIM MEYERS

Jim is consulting, training, and learning from nationals in the Caleb and Joshua Foundation (a member of the Wycliffe Global Alliance) in Southeast Asia. He and his wife, Heather, feel privileged to be part of the Bible translation movement happening in four language groups which includes Sunday school curriculum, Bible study booklets, and oral Bible storying.

ANDY MINCH

When Andy and his wife, Audrey, answered God's call to Bible translation over thirty years ago, they never dreamed what he had in store. They joined with the Amanab people of Papua New Guinea, providing the expertise to translate Scriptures into that language. Today Andy serves as an international administrator overseeing the academic services that support Bible translation in the Pacific area of the world.

DUSTIN MOODY

Dustin has traveled to the Congo, the Philippines, and Papua New Guinea to discover and share stories of lives transformed through God's Word. After serving with Wycliffe for eight years, he believes that God speaks every language, and that Bible translation is the best way for those still waiting to hear from him firsthand.

BONNIE NYSTROM

Bonnie and her husband, John, joined the Bible translation ministry more than thirty years ago. Much of their service has been with the Aitape West translation project in Papua New Guinea. Bonnie and John are authors of *Sleeping Coconuts*, which recounts how God used a devastating tsunami to expand the Aitape West translation project from translation work in one language to involve eleven language communities. Bonnie has also served in leadership in several organizations in the Bible translation movement.

KEITH PATMAN

Keith lived in the Gunu community in Cameroon from 1987 to 1995 and helped them launch their Bible translation program. He made return visits in 2013 and 2014 to check the final books of the New Testament. He continues to serve the language communities of francophone Africa through writing Bible translation guides in French and traveling to Africa twice a year to check translated Scripture.

TODD PETERSON

Todd was an NFL placekicker. Upon graduating from the University of Georgia he was drafted by the New York Giants in 1993 and retired in 2006; his last team was his hometown Atlanta Falcons. He formerly chaired Wycliffe's affiliate, the Seed Company. Todd and his wife, Susan, have a deep sense of personal value for God's Word. Together they are faithful advocates of the Bible translation movement.

SUE PFAFF

Sue continues to find that her life as a Bible translator in Papua New Guinea has been an amazing adventure, and a significant part of that adventure has been seeing how the power of God's Word influences and changes lives. She and her husband, Jerry, have been serving the Nali people of Manus Island since 1987.

JACK POPJES

Jack and his wife, Jo, worked together with the Canela people of Brazil for twenty-two years to train literacy teachers and produce a government-approved alphabet, learn-to-read materials, and a partial Bible—250 pages of the Old Testament and 500 pages of the New Testament. "This feels like the greatest day in my life," Jack said on the day they distributed this Bible.

DON RICHARDSON

Don is a missionary statesman, best-selling author, and artist who teaches worldwide on topics related to missions and cultures. He is minister-at-large for World Team, the mission under whom he served for fifteen years in Papua, Indonesia, among the cannibal-headhunter Sawi community. He helped translate the New Testament into Sawi and render the tribe literate. Don has authored seven books, including *Peace Child* and *Eternity in Their Hearts*, and helped produce two missionary films, *Peace Child* and *Never the Same*.

GABRIEL AND JEANETTE SALGUERO

Revs. Gabriel and Jeanette are pastors of Calvario Church in Orlando, Florida. They are the cofounders of the National Latino Evangelical Coalition, which serves three thousand Hispanic evangelical congregations. They have served as missionaries in Africa, Asia, and Latin America.

CAROL SCHATZ

Carol helped facilitate the New Testament translation for the Teribe people of Panama. She and her husband, Larry, have dedicated more than forty years to the ministry of Bible translation. Today Carol assists Wycliffe USA's president and CEO, Bob Creson, and enjoys gathering stories from around the world about the transformative work God is doing through Bible translation.

TERRILL SCHROCK

From 2008 to 2016, Terrill and his wife, Amber, worked among the Ik people in northeast Uganda in linguistics, language development, and health care. Their holistic approach to ministry took on a new dimension in the adoption of two Ik girls. Terrill is passionate about loving people through language, and Amber, about alleviating people's suffering.

WENDY SCOTT-PENSON

Derwin and Wendy have worked with Wycliffe Bible Translators for years, educating the public about Bible translation. Wendy and Derwin have been married for twenty-six years and have three adopted children.

HILDEGARD SEILER

Hildegard received a call from the Lord to serve the Eskimos. She and her husband, Wolf, dedicated their lives in Bible translation working with the Inupiaq people in Alaska. After completing their New Testament, songbook, and dictionary, the Seilers transitioned to translation workshops and Scripture checking in Nigeria and Zambia for eleven years. Hildegard retired in 2015 after forty-five years of service with Wycliffe.

STEVE SHELDON

Steve is a former executive director of SIL International and Wycliffe Bible Translators International (now the Wycliffe Global Alliance). He helped document one of Brazil's minority languages, and promoted involvement of both Brazilians and indigenous peoples in the Bible translation movement. In the early 1960s God spoke to Steve and his wife, Linda, through the J. B. Phillips New Testament in Modern English for Students. They couldn't imagine life without God's Word.

JULIE SHIMER

Julie has thirty years combined experience in leadership at several major corporations such as Welch Allyn, Motorola, Inc., AT&T Bell Laboratories, and Bethlehem Steel Company. But Julie is passionate about more than just business. She's been captivated by what God is doing through Bible translation ever since the first time she heard a Wycliffe missionary speak at a church service, and continues to be an advocate for this ministry today.

CAROL SISSEL

Carol and her husband, Tim, have served the Bible translation ministry in Mexico for almost twenty years. Carol has been involved with desktop publishing, manuscript editing, and currently, she is helping prepare Scripture apps for Android devices.

DANIELLE SMITH

Danielle met her husband, Michael, while training to be a Bible translator at the Global Institute for Applied Linguistics in Texas. They have worked in Vanuatu since 2009, where they are facilitating a translation in one of the country's one hundred-plus vernacular languages, Motlap, which has about two thousand speakers. Danielle currently spends most of her time homeschooling and caring for their three young children.

ATUL TANDON

Atul is a global entrepreneur and humanitarian who helps social enterprises achieve sustainability and scalability as rapidly as possible. He's the founder of Tandon Institute and former executive director of United Way Worldwide's International Network. where he led the world's largest charity group, striving to advance the common good at the community level.

WILLIAM CAMERON TOWNSEND

The man who started it all! Cameron began his journey toward Bible translation as a Bible salesman in Guatemala. He quickly realized no one was interested in the Spanish Bibles he was trying to sell, because they didn't speak the language. He set out to make Scripture available to minority language speakers, and eventually founded Wycliffe Bible Translators and SIL International to facilitate translation and literacy for those people groups.

JOHN WATTERS

John was the executive director and later president of SIL International, one of Wycliffe's primary partners, which serves people groups worldwide in sustainable language development, including Bible translation. He and his wife, Kathie, have spent forty-five years serving God in linguistics, translation, literacy, and Scripture engagement, including many years with language groups in Cameroon and Nigeria.

ANNE WEST

Anne dedicated fifty years of her life to serving in Bible translation before retiring in 2015. She ministered to the people in the Philippines in the areas of literacy, translation, and administration.

PATRICIA WILKENDORF

Patricia helped facilitate the translation of the Nomaande New Testament in Cameroon. She then worked as a consultant with six other neighboring language communities, all in the Mbam region of central Cameroon. Since 2015 Patricia has been living in Dallas, working as a resource coordinator on the Wycliffe USA Care Team to help fellow missionaries who are going through transitions.

RACHEL YANAC

Rachel, her husband, Ade, and their two sons live in the Andes Mountains of Peru, where they help minority language groups apply newly translated Scripture and other resources to their everyday life and culture. Rachel credits a missionary family from her childhood church with introducing her to the work of Bible translation, and Ade feels privileged to be bringing God's Word to his own people in their heart language.

FORREST ZANDER

As a missionary pilot, Forrey has flown to and from some of the most remote places on earth, carrying people and supplies to support the work God is doing around the world. Together he and his late wife, Margaret, have dedicated over fifty years to ministry with Wycliffe. Forrey is the author of *His Faithfulness Reaches to the Skies,* about his experiences as a pilot and in other roles promoting Bible translation.

THANK YOU

EDITOR

Katie Kuykendall

DESIGN & ILLUSTRATION

Ben Rupp

COPY EDITORS

Angela Burleigh

Mary Calvez

Leigh DeVore

Carol Schatz

FULFILLMENT

Margaret Coyle

Kristie Frieze

Kathy Zoetewey

PHOTOGRAPHY

Rodney Ballard

Gustavo Barral

Joseph Barrientos

Colton Brown

Aaron Burden

Andrew Coelho

Dikaseva

Kien Do

Zachary Domes

Hans Eiskonen

Jared Erondu

Marc Ewell

Patrick Fore

Francesco Gallarotti

Alexa Gaul

Jake Givens

Anna Goncharova

Frances Gunn

Lara Natalia Haenny

Rosan Harmens

Alex Hockett

Eric Huang

Viktor Jakovlev

Peter Kent

Rodion Kutsaev

Katie Kuykendall

Dominik Lange

Thomas Lefebvre

Henry Lo

Peter John Maridable

Silvestri Matteo

Nitish Meena

Levi Morsy

Dyaa Eldin Moustafa

Georg Nietsch

Clem Onojeghuo

Cagatay Orhan

Luís Perdigão

Andrew Ridley

Alice Donovan Rouse

Ben Rupp

Samuel Scrimshaw

Shontz Photography

Aliis Sinisalu

Ivan Slade

Matthew Smith

Samantha Sophia

Joshua Sortino

Kyle Szegedi

Jeremy Thomas

Alexey Topolyanskiy

Daniel Lozano Valdés

Thong Vo

Jan Erik Waider

Rémi Walle

Jordan Whitt

Christian Widell

Will van Wingerden

Charles Yeager

Luca Zanon

Filip Zrnzević

VISIT US

wycliffe.org

CONNECT

@wycliffeusa

SAY HELLO

info@wycliffe.org

ISAIAH 51:20
461
and I will make my judgment to rest for a light of the
HOLY
BIBLE